# DEDICATION

For our parents
who sacrificed,
inspired us to aim higher,
and were examples of leading
with love and purpose—
and for every parent
helping the next generation
become more.

Jason & Jennifer Eubanks

A PARENT'S SURVIVAL GUIDE
TO THE COLLEGE YEARS

# TUITION, TAILGATES AND TEARS

## WHERE YOU'LL MAJOR IN LETTING GO AND MINOR IN KEEPING IT TOGETHER

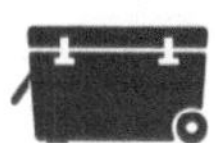

REAL TALK FROM PARENTS WHO JUGGLED THREE KIDS, THREE COLLEGES, AND ALL THE CHAOS IN BETWEEN

Jason and Jennifer Eubanks

ISBN: 979-8-9958515-0-9
Published by Eubanks Press
Printed in the United States of America
*Written by Jason Eubanks, with contributions from Jennifer Eubanks*
*Cover design by Aaron Branding*
*Creative direction by Jason Eubanks*
*Interior design and typesetting by Conectiv*
*Edited by Dr. Ehren Jarrett*

For the moms holding it together
at the dorm, then losing it three steps
into their kids' empty bedroom.

For the dads who play it cool all day,
then tear up folding a left-behind hoodie.

For the couples staring across
the dinner table thinking,

So... now what?

## TABLE OF CONTENTS

# FOREWORD/PREFACE

When your first child goes off to college, you think it's just their big leap. It's not. It's yours, too.

We didn't know it then, standing in a dorm room surrounded by bins, bedding, and a futon we couldn't quite assemble without losing our cool, but sending our kids to college was about to change our lives as much as theirs.

Over the span of six years, we launched three kids into three different universities: University of Iowa, University of Alabama, and University of Missouri. For us, that meant two high school graduation parties (twins), three dorm move-ins, a dozen apartment leases, countless Target runs, and more tailgates than our livers care to remember. We've rented moving trucks and trailers in multiple states, booked hotel rooms a full year in advance, and spent entire weekends trying not to embarrass ourselves (or our kids) at bars where we were easily twice the average age.

We've also done the hard parts: the long drives home after drop-off in complete silence, the late-night "Can you Venmo me?" texts, and the learning curve of giving them space when we really wanted to ask a hundred questions. We've learned what it feels like to see them struggle, and the pride that comes when they figure it out without you.

This book is the guide we wish someone had handed us before we started. Equal parts survival manual, pep talk, and insider playbook. It's filled with what really happens when your kid goes to college: the unspoken rules of campus visits, the truth about Greek life dues, the right way to tailgate without being that parent, and the emotional whiplash of watching them grow up while you're learning how to let go.

We've written it together, Mom and Dad, because we often saw the same moments differently. One of us noticed the tearful hugs in the driveway, the first texts home, and the way their dorm rooms reflected who they were becoming. The other remembers the logistics, the bar tabs, and the tailgate grill that got used exactly once. Between us, you'll get both sides: the heart and the humor, the tips and the trip-ups.

Whether you're counting down to drop-off, deep in the chaos, or looking back with hard-earned wisdom, we hope these pages make you feel understood, make you laugh, stir up some good memories, and make the ride a little smoother.

Because college isn't just their story.
It's yours, too.

— Jason & Jennifer Eubanks

# INTRODUCTION

You've been parenting for 18 years. You've handled diapers, carpools, ballgames, competitions, science fair projects, late-night fevers, and every curveball a teenager can throw at you. But nothing quite prepares you for the moment your child packs their life into a stack of plastic bins and a few oversized IKEA FRAKTA bags, flashes a nervous smile, and says, "Okay, I'm ready."

Sending a kid to college isn't just about getting them there, it's about stepping into a brand-new role yourself. One that comes with no manual, no off switch, and more than a few years of figuring it out as you go. It's part cheerleader, part safety net, part ATM, and part quiet observer who's learning how to let go without disappearing.

That's where this book comes in. It's not a lecture from a parenting expert, it's a companion for the road ahead. A mix of humor, honesty, and the kind of real-world details you only get from living it: the unexpected rules of visiting, how to stay connected without crowding them, and why the best memories often happen somewhere between the tailgate tent and the drive home.

Think of it as a field guide for one of the weirdest, most emotional, most unexpectedly fun jobs you'll ever have: being a college parent. The pay is terrible, the hours are unpredictable, but the rewards, like watching them grow and learning who you are without them under your roof, are worth every bit of the chaos.

## CHAPTER ONE

# The Countdown Begins

## (Now It's Real)

The truth is, no one's ever really ready.

Not for the planning. Not for the packing. Not for the silence that hits after the goodbye. One minute you're helping them tie their shoes. The next, you're crying in the driveway, wondering where the time went.

Let's rewind.

They narrowed college options down to a few. You joined them on the tours. You asked all the questions, some intelligent, some purely logistical ("How far is this from Target?"). You smiled and nodded while your kid juggled the info between texts and snaps during campus visits, until they saw the rec center. Suddenly, they had opinions.

Our son toured a few schools that fit his interests.

University of Illinois at Chicago (UIC)? Too much city.

Augustana? Liked it but didn't love it.

But then we walked the campus at the University of Iowa. Kinnick. Downtown. Campus Rec. The black-and-gold energy of Iowa City. The programs. The opportunities. That was it. He lit up. We knew. It would be his new home.

And when that "You're in!" email finally hits, complete with a personalized video of Herky the Hawk holding signs with your kid's name on them, it's official. Instant goosebumps.

The emotional roller coaster has officially left the station. Strap yourself in.

But before you get to the hard part, like saying goodbye, there's a high school grad party to plan. Because nothing screams "My baby's leaving me" like a rented tent, a slideshow of childhood photos, catered food, signature cocktails, and a custom Snapchat filter decked out in their new school colors.

His was a black-and-gold bash worthy of a Big Ten sendoff, with cupcakes, napkins, and cookies all Hawkeye-themed. We spent hours on a playlist curation like we were DJing for Coachella: Class of 2019 Edition. There was a slideshow too, complete with endless photos from K–12, which included late nights piecing it together, and more tears than we ever expected as the early years played back in front of us.

And while the party looked picture-perfect, reality had other plans.

At our son's grad party, we learned two valuable lessons: teens are crafty, and parents age ten years hosting one of these things. We'd done everything right. The food was great, the playlist was rolling, the adults were having a good time, and the kids were hanging out in every corner of the yard.

Around 11 p.m., just when things were winding down, I started seeing more activity. Turns out, one of the kids, ironically, the son of a close family friend, had shown up with a backpack full of "supplies" and a youthful belief that Snapchat invitations are harmless. Within minutes, random kids we knew and others we didn't know started showing up. Apparently, a "party's just getting started" message went out to sixty plus in a group chat.

Next thing we know, we've got uninvited guests crawling in basement windows while we're trying to shut things down. We tracked down the source, had a nice little "chat," and minimized the damage. Looking back, it was the perfect preview of college life, full of good intentions, bad decisions, and lessons learned the hard way.

Two years later, we doubled the fun (and doubled the cost) when our twin daughters picked Alabama and Mizzou. Crimson and white clashed gloriously with black-and-gold. We went all out with bag boards customized for each school, a food truck, and one giant, beautiful memory well documented in the 100-photo social media dump we swore we would keep simple.

We thought we'd learned from that first one. We hadn't.

Our goal was same concept, bigger scale. Two schools, two themes, twice the chaos. Mother Nature, however, had other plans.

The week before the party, Northern Illinois went through an identity crisis and tried to become Arizona. Spoiler: it nailed it. Temperatures hit nearly 100 degrees, and our irrigation system quit on us. Mostly because our well was running dry and needed to be drilled deeper. My once-perfect Kentucky bluegrass, lush, striped, and the pride of the neighborhood, was turning crispy brown by the hour. The well guy couldn't get to us until after the party, which meant we were about to host a backyard bash on what looked like scorched earth. In nearly twenty years of living there, the yard had never looked so bad.

By party day, it hit 100 degrees sharp, as if Mother Nature RSVP'd "Oh, I'm coming, and I'm bringing heat.

I lost about ten pounds just setting up. Guests were drinking faster than we could restock coolers and the bartenders could sling cocktails. I greeted everyone with a hand towel over my shoulder just to wipe the sweat off my brow like some kind of suburban boxer between rounds.

The party still turned out great, but my lawn didn't recover for weeks. Parenthood, I've learned, will test your patience, your pride, and your sprinkler system, all before college even starts.

When the last tent came down and the coolers were finally empty, we caught our breath and realized the party was a hit, even if the yard looked like a desert. But just like the grass, not everything goes according to plan.

One of our daughters had dreamed of cheering at Bama, but when tryouts went virtual, that path shifted. At that level, everyone who makes it to finals is incredibly talented, and the difference often comes down to relationships and connection. That's tough to build when everyone is in masks and the world is shut down. Still, she chose Alabama and built her own version of the dream.

It was one of many moments that didn't go exactly as planned.

> **Mom's Take:** Let's be honest, those graduation parties are usually powered by mom's with Pinterest boards, Amazon carts, and just enough Prosecco to survive it. I spent more time choosing cupcakes and napkins than I did on our wedding. Themed cocktails? Done. Matching balloons? Absolutely. Did anyone thank me? Not really. But when I saw them smiling, surrounded by friends and family, I knew, this was our sendoff, too.

> **Dad's Pro Tip:** You will not make money on this party. This is not a fundraiser. It's a farewell. The kids get the cards and cash. You get the receipts and maybe a thank-you text, if you're lucky. But you also get this quiet realization: this whole college thing? It's officially happening.

It's after the party when reality sets in.

If you were a financial rock star with a fully loaded 529 plan, we salute you. If you're like us? We had a little 529, but not nearly enough to cover three kids, three schools, and three sets of "must-have" dorm essentials. Thankfully, we made it through without taking out parent loans, using one creatively rebalanced budget, some reduced funding in our retirement plan, a few blessedly good business years between and a whole lot of faith that it would somehow work out.

Our kids took the loans they qualified for. We picked up "the rest."

And that "rest"? It quietly took on a life of its own in spirit wear, tailgate gear, Venmo requests, and splurges on last-minute essentials like portable grills and Yeti coolers.

And here's the kicker. Just when you're starting to feel overwhelmed, you catch yourself getting pumped. Because college becomes your identity, too. Tailgates. Parent weekends. Spirit wear in your size. You're basically going back to college without the homework, but with twice the costs and half the metabolism.

My wife and I graduated SIU (Southern Illinois University) where we met in the early '90s. One of the top party schools in the country at the time, with nearly 25,000 students and a basketball team that could hold its own. But it certainly wasn't the Big Ten or SEC. It wasn't black-and-gold Saturdays or nationally televised game days.

It was also more than 30 years ago. No social media. No Pinterest dorm boards. No roommate-finding apps. College today feels louder, more curated, and less analog, with everything seemingly TikTok- or Instagram-worthy.

That's part of what makes this transition hit so hard. You're not just saying goodbye to your kid, you're saying goodbye to your version of college, too.

Right when worries start stacking up, bam, it's dorm room time.

Cue the Amazon frenzy.

Pretty soon, your front porch looks like a shipping depot. Mattress pads. Desk lamps. Command hooks. Tapestries that are apparently "a vibe." You've officially moved from "essentials only" to "HGTV mini-makeover." Boys seem to be easier: gray sheets, a university flag on the wall, a mini fridge, and a microwave. Done.

Girls? It's a Pinterest board come to life. Headboards, LED

lights, IKEA drawer units repurposed into "custom" setups, and color schemes that somehow require 47 Online orders and a mild drinking habit to complete.

And if they've got a roommate? It becomes a full-blown logistics operation. "Who's bringing what?" "Do our comforters match?" "Will their vibe ruin my aesthetic?" Oh, and the shared living room? Yeah, brace yourself. Dorms have those now. Ours didn't have to navigate the matching comforter drama. They each had their own bedroom within a four-person suite, while still sharing the bathrooms, kitchen, and living room.

At first, you say you're just helping. Then you realize… you're all in.

Because beneath the to-do lists and Target runs, the reality is hitting you. They're leaving. Like, for real. Not to a sleepover or a summer camp, but to a new chapter where you're not the center anymore. And suddenly, you're not exactly invited, even though you're paying for it.

In that moment, it hits you. This isn't just their education. It's yours too. You're starting your degree in letting go, with a minor in keeping it together. A course no one prepares you for, with exams you never see coming.

And what follows might just be the hardest, funniest, most emotional unpaid internship of your life.

Being a college parent.

Welcome to prep season. You're already behind.

**Mom's Pro Tip:** Join the freshman parent Facebook groups for your university. They're mostly parents asking questions and other parents answering them, which can be genuinely helpful for dorm life, move-in, and how things work. Just be prepared for the occasional helicopter-parent post that makes you think, "Your kid is 18, not 10." Or the opinionated parent who says anything behind a screen, convinced their take is the only correct one. Just put on your ignore hat, take it all with a grain of salt, and use the group for the solid info it offers.

CHAPTER TWO

# The Great Dorm Outfitting Debacle

It starts innocent enough.

"We'll just get the essentials."

Cut to three weeks later: you've got boxes from Amazon, Target, and Bed Bath & Beyond stacked so high you can't find your dog anymore. You've bought things you've never heard of, half of them requiring a YouTube tutorial to figure out, and somehow you still feel like you're forgetting something important.

Let's start with the basics:

- **Mattress topper:** the most expensive slice of foam you'll ever buy, but a must
- **Command strips and hooks:** more precious than gold during dorm move-in
- **Mini fridge:** a must-have, even though it'll mostly hold energy drinks and takeout
- **Microwave:** for late-night ramen, popcorn, and

occasionally reheating something that resembles food

- **Laundry basket:** which will remain decorative until Thanksgiving

They swear they're keeping it simple. Then one TikTok dorm room tour sends them into a full spiral: string lights, area rugs, makeup desks with lighted mirrors, matching bedside lamps and inspirational wall quotes. Back in our day, the décor peaked at a Bob Marley poster from Spencer's taped to a cinderblock wall.

Planning for twin girls in two different states with completely different styles? That's a full-blown HGTV season. One wanted neutrals combined with animal print; the other was all about blush tones and bold accents. There were headboards, IKEA drawer units, rugs, matching lamps, and carefully curated throw pillows. They designed every detail like their dorm was going to be featured in a magazine. And honestly, they kind of nailed it.

> **Mom's Pro Tip:** Grab those oversized IKEA moving bags on Amazon. Doesn't have to be the real deal, the knockoffs hold just as much chaos. You'll use them for everything and wonder how you ever lived without them.

Dads turn into logistics managers. You're tracking shipments like it's your side hustle. You start dropping terms like "optimal layout" and "modular storage," obsessing over whether the drawer unit will fit under the lofted bed and if a shoe shelf or hanging rack is the smarter play.

And just when you think you'll save some money by splitting items with their roommate in the common areas?

Wrong. They'll talk it through, make a plan, and still both buy the same things. Apparently, nobody trusts anyone else's definition of 'good quality.'

> **Dad's Pro Tip:** Set up a Google Sheet to track what you've bought. At first it feels like you're in control. In reality, you're not. You start with the essentials, but by the end the list has quadrupled and includes things you didn't even know existed.

By the time you're actually packing the car or renting a U-Haul, you've got bins labeled, extension cords coiled, moving bags ready, and a mental checklist running on repeat.

For us, it felt like outfitting a small studio apartment. I ran point on style. At least for our son's dorm, that was my department. My wife made sure no detail got overlooked and still managed to sneak in extra orders where she could. She's the checklist queen and didn't want to miss a thing. Thankfully, this move didn't involve an IKEA drawer unit. But I would go on to build more of those than I can count, and now, when I can, I travel with a tool kit like it's part of my parenting license.

Two years later when we got to Alabama, we thought we were seasoned pros. We had the move-in time, the checklist, the plan. We pulled up in our rented 15-passenger van, and before we could even open the doors, a small army of student volunteers swooped in and started unloading every bin and bag into rolling carts. It was a full-service operation. College kids moving other college kids into college. I wasn't sure whether to help or just applaud.

Our daughter was in one of the high-rise Presidential dorms on the far side of campus, higher floor, thankfully with a working elevator. Her roommates had earlier move-in slots, so by the time we arrived the main kitchen and living room area already looked like a small storage unit. Some of those boxes were ours. They'd been hauled over from our Airbnb by one of the roommate's dads, who had driven everything down from northern Illinois. We'd flown into Birmingham, which meant no tools, except the trusty starter toolkit I'd bought each kid when they left home.

> **Dad's Pro Tip:** Buy a small toolkit for every kid when they move out. Ours lived in their dorm and apartment closets all four years. By senior year, a few tools were missing or broken, but that was proof they'd actually used them.

My job was simple: carry, assemble, repeat, then get out of the way once the decorating decisions started flying. My daughter had been planning that part for months and I knew when to stay out of the way. At one point, I escaped to grab sandwiches for everyone. The next morning, I grabbed the keys for a quick coffee run before finishing the last few move-in details and accidentally drove right through Sorority Row during prep week. I turned onto the street and was instantly surrounded by what looked like hundreds of girls, same height, same age, same blonde hair, same energy. All walking shoulder to shoulder, crossing in front of me toward Starbucks for their morning caffeine before prep sessions. The place was about to look like a casting call for "Legally Blonde: The Sequel," and I wasn't waiting behind 300 iced caramel macchiatos with oat milk. I made a quick u-turn and found coffee elsewhere.

Back at the dorm, the air-conditioning felt like divine intervention. Four sets of parents, all equally sweaty and sentimental, worked side by side, trying not to make eye contact when the reality hit: we'd be heading home soon, and they wouldn't be coming with us. That's the thing about move-in day. It's half triumph, half heartbreak.

Before we left, we reminded our daughter about the tornado shelter next door, just in case. She only used it once, but I got what felt like weekly automated tornado warning calls for the next four years. Turns out Tuscaloosa has way more rain, and way more storms, than I ever imagined.

When everything was finally in place, we took the last photo, our daughter standing on the sidewalk in front of her high-rise dorm, smiling in the Alabama sun, ready to begin her new life. That picture still gets me every time.

We thought we'd seen it all, until the Mizzou move-in. We discovered a new definition of "overpacking." Our daughter didn't just bring what she needed for college, she brought what she'd need to colonize a new planet.

Her logic was simple: "I might need it." Apparently, that included every throw pillow, pair of shoes, piece of clothing, and knickknack she owned. By the time we loaded the moving truck, it looked less like freshman move-in and more like a cross-country relocation.

When we finally got everything into her dorm, it was wall-to-wall. You couldn't tell where the storage bins ended and the décor began. The only thing we ended up taking back home was her electric guitar and amp, because it literally wouldn't fit in the room.

Moving them into their new life is a lot of work, but there's something beautiful about watching it all come together. The excitement on their face. The effort they put in. This space, roughly the size of a walk-in closet, somehow becomes their whole world.

You'll step back, take a few photos of them in their new space, and probably tear up when they say, "It's perfect." Just don't forget the batteries. Or the surge protector. Or the tools to hang the flatscreen. Or the protein snacks. Always bring snacks. Everyone's so dialed in to finish moving in that there's no time to get food.

CHAPTER THREE

# The Lasts You Didn't Know Were Lasts

No one warns you about the "lasts." Not the big ones like graduation, dorm drop-off, or the final dinner before goodbye. You see those coming.

It's the quiet ones that sneak up.

The last time you remind them to clear the half-empty water bottles from their room. The last time you remind them, again, to put away the laundry you folded and left in the hallway.

What feels like annoyances in the moment are actually rituals. They're the ordinary parts of parenting you didn't know you were savoring until they were suddenly gone.

And then there's the last time you kick up a favorite playlist and everyone somehow ends up in the same room, passing around popcorn and stories from the week. You don't know it's a goodbye to something small but sacred. The easy kind of togetherness that disappears before you even realize it mattered.

The week before move-in hits like a freight train. You want to hit pause. All at once, you're trying to cram in all the parenting you forgot to do: life advice, laundry lessons, grocery shopping 101, and sermonizing on the importance of sleep. You start suggesting game nights, pedicure outings, and ice cream runs like you're auditioning for "Parent of the Year.

Meanwhile, your kid is booked and buzzing with group chats, goodbye plans, and last-minute Target runs. They're halfway out the door already. And you're desperately clinging to what's right now.

And that stings.

For moms, it's a tug of war between wanting to hold on and wanting them to be ready. You're folding their laundry for the last time, hoping you remembered to teach them enough. How to do the wash, make a meal, or just make good choices. For dads, it hits in the quiet moments. You start noticing the house feels different already. The transition is underway. It's a strange energy, like packing the day before a vacation, only this trip comes with a little emptiness. The countdown is no longer measured in days but in lasts.

While you're replaying their baby pictures in your head, they're trying on a whole new life.

You'll find yourself watching them more that week, trying to memorize what normal looks like. The way they walk through the kitchen. The sound of their car pulling into the driveway. You start to realize how much of your everyday life has revolved around their rhythm, and that rhythm is about to change.

> **Mom's Pro Tip:** Don't try to fill every moment. They'll be busy saying their own goodbyes and closing out their lasts with friends. Just be there. The most meaningful ones happen when you least expect them.

Even younger siblings feel it. The house energy shifts. Everyone's a little quieter, trying to figure out what life will sound like when one of you isn't there every day. It's not sadness exactly, it's awareness. A new chapter beginning for all of you.

That last week is a blur of logistics, emotions, and trying not to cry in public. You realize this transition isn't just theirs. It's yours, too. It's letting go in pieces, one coffee chat, one grocery run, one goodbye hug at a time.

What helped us?

What mattered most was making the effort to show up. To grab the last-minute lunch. To toss the football. To sit on the couch even when no one was really talking. To watch them pack the bins and bite your tongue when they were clearly doing it wrong.

> **Dad's Pro Tip:** Make the first move. It's easy for dads to fill their time with work or projects just to stay out of the way, and sometimes it's to suppress the real emotion. Be there. They do want you around. Plan a donut run. Ask them to grab their mitt and play catch or go see a movie. You're not just making memories; you're showing them what it looks like to be present. Even if the moment makes that lump in your throat a little bigger.

Those last weeks and days will leave an imprint on all of you. It's the little things that stay with you. The sounds, the glances, the quiet in-between moments you don't realize matter until later.

Some memories stand out forever. Like the day of the move, when we watched our son stare quietly out the window on the ride to Iowa, and it hit us that he was feeling it, too. Two years later, in the driveway, our twin daughters shared a long, tearful embrace goodbye before the first one left for Alabama. We captured it on video, and we still can't watch it without tearing up.

Here's what we'll tell you: you don't get to pick the final moments. You just have to show up for them. Be there, even when they act like they don't want you to be. Especially then.

Because even if they don't say it, they notice.

They always notice.

## CHAPTER FOUR

# The Family Talk — Money, Safety and Laundry

Somewhere between the last thank-you note and the dorm move-in checklist, it hits you: there are still real-life conversations you haven't had yet. Not just the sentimental ones, but the "how to not fall apart out there" ones.

These talks aren't glamorous. They don't come with a photo op. But they matter. So, we broke them down into three categories, each one worthy of a driveway chat, a coffee run, or a late-night kitchen counter conversation.

### Money: AKA, The Venmo Vortex

Let's be real, college is expensive, and most of the budget talks happen on the fly. We didn't have a perfect system, but we did have rules. Groceries, gas for visits home, and essentials? We paid. Uber rides? If it kept them from driving after drinking, we covered it without question. But they needed to factor that cost into their night out from the start. Late-night snacks and cocktails with friends? Not our department.

We remember one of our daughters Venmo-requesting money for "educational supplies." Naturally, we sent it. Later, we learned it was for self-tanner. Another time, a "Target essentials" trip somehow included throw pillows and a new curling iron. They weren't trying to pull one over on us, just creatively redefining the word "need."

We always knew kids were clever, but we encountered a few fresh attempts at padding their bank accounts. They'd pay for each other's meals, Venmo each other behind the scenes, and hope we wouldn't notice so we'd cover the whole thing. Once we caught on, we set limits. "Here's fifteen bucks for dinner. Make it work." It became the norm. They got creative, and we stayed mostly sane.

Set a weekly budget. Make it livable but not luxurious. You want to help, of course. But you also want them to feel the weight of money a little. Not to stress them out, but to help them think.

Better they learn how to budget now than bounce rent later.

We weren't trying to turn them into accountants. We just wanted them to know the difference between "need" and "nice to have." After freshman year, we nudged them to get a job, whether it was on campus, at a restaurant, behind a bar, at a country club, or anywhere they could earn a few bucks. Not because we couldn't help, but because a $28 sushi order and a 1 a.m. Uber Eats delivery hit harder when it's your own money and you've just spent five hours clearing tables while listening to Yacht Rock on repeat. That's when a bank balance stops being abstract and starts teaching lessons.

> **Dad's Pro Tip:** If your kid texts, "Can I get $20 for food?" check the bank statement first. Odds are, they already blew their food budget on Xbox credits… and now they're actually hungry. We called these teachable moments. The truth is, our kids rarely asked for money, and we usually knew what they had left. As parents, we didn't want them going without. We'd rather they focus on school than stress about being too broke to eat or join their friends. Most of the time, you'll know when it's really needed, and that's when we'd send a little comfort money their way.

**Safety: "Don't Walk Alone" and Other Broken Records**

This one is hard because it feels like a lecture. And let's be honest, most of us repeat ourselves like we're trying to win an award for "Most Anxious Parent."

With our son, the talk focused on awareness. Know your surroundings. Watch out for your friends. Know when to walk away. Always have a plan. Nothing good happens after midnight.

With our daughters, the talk was more intense. Stick together. Watch your drink. Don't scroll through your phone while walking across campus. Keep your head up. Trust your gut.

And for all of them: always, always call us. No matter what. No judgment. No lecture. Just call.

Yes, we did the whole "Find My iPhone" and Life360 thing. We pay for the phones and the service, so it wasn't up for debate. Our son wasn't on Life360, mostly due to timing. It wasn't on our radar until after he turned 16, and by then, we were already using Find My iPhone, so we didn't push it.

They groaned. We held firm. Boundaries came later. Peace of mind came first.

Honestly, these talks weren't just for them. They were for us too. To feel like we had done our part. To quiet the voice in our head that whispers worst-case scenarios at 2 a.m. Even if the only time they truly listened was when we whispered one last reminder before leaving the dorm and heading back home.

My wife remembers giving our daughter "the talk" before she left for school, rattling off every safety rule known to humankind. She listened patiently, nodding the way kids do when they want to make you feel like you've been heard. A few weeks later, she texted after walking back from class: "Made it home safe." That was it. No heart emoji. No follow-up. My wife just stared at that message like it was gold. It wasn't about control, it was about connection. She'd listened after all.

> **Mom's Pro Tip:** Say what you need to say, even if it feels like nagging. They might roll their eyes, but they hear you. And when they do the thing you hoped they would, even just once, you'll exhale with relief and know your words stayed with them.

### Laundry: The Final Frontier

Eighteen years of doing most of the folding, stacking, and sorting, and now it's their turn. Sort of.

We walked through the basics. Don't mix whites and reds. Don't overload the washer or dryer. Don't leave your wet stuff in the washer until it smells like a forgotten gym sock. Use an iron or at least a steamer. We armed them with detergent pods, dryer sheets, and clear instructions.

Did they listen? Kind of. Did they bring it all home anyway? Every single time.

When one of the girls came home that first long weekend, she lugged in duffel bags so heavy they could count as gym equipment. Inside was what looked like her entire college wardrobe, and not a single clean item in the bunch. I'm still not sure how she managed to wear everything without running out of clothes or friends.

We laughed, rolled up our sleeves, and started sorting like old times. Somewhere between the spin cycle and the folding table, it hit us: they're going to be fine.

Here's the truth we learned, especially from Mom's side of the launch. They know more than we think. And even if they mess it up, they'll figure it out. Laundry mishaps aren't life-threatening. They're part of growing up.

And that's really what this stage is about, passing along the small lessons that prepare them for the bigger ones.

> **Dad's Pro Tip:** If your kid is taking a car to school, connect with a reliable local mechanic before they need one. That way, when the "check engine" light comes on or they clip a curb and blow a tire, they're not Googling random repair shops in a panic. Bonus points if you introduce yourself to the mechanic in advance and store their number in your kid's phone. In a college town, a trustworthy shop is priceless peace of mind.

### Final Thought Before Move-In

We considered making a laminated, color-coded checklist of the essentials: logins and passwords, emergency contacts, laundry instructions, basically everything short of a survival guide for the apocalypse.

They would have humored us, maybe even thanked us, and then left it in a drawer they never opened. So, we kept it simple. Communicate the important stuff. Put a few key pieces into a shared Google Doc. Then, hoped some of it stuck.

Because no matter how independent they act, they still need you.

And no matter how much you think you've taught them, you'll still want to teach them one more thing.

Keep the talks short. Keep your voice steady. And leave room for them to ask what they need, even if they roll their eyes.

You're not just prepping them to do life alone. You're reminding them you'll always be there, even from the sidelines.

Because this is the moment you shift from full-time parent to part-time guide. Still on the team, just in a new position.

## CHAPTER FIVE

# Drop-Off Day – How to Not Lose It (Completely)

There's no way around it. This is the moment you've been both planning for and quietly dreading: the day you drop them off.

If you're lucky, your university gives you a scheduled time to move in. It helps with traffic, crowd control, and emotional denial. You've had piles of stuff stacked in the rarely used dining room for weeks, a room that mostly sees action on holidays. You've rented the bigger vehicle or a moving truck. Maybe both. And now it's go time.

Packing the car is like playing the world's most expensive game of Tetris. Every bin, box, lamp, and flatscreen is perfectly placed. You check the list twice. That walk back inside for one last check hits you; the house already feels weirdly empty. You pause, refuse to let your thoughts go too deep, then head out the door. And just like that, you're pulling out of the driveway.

There's excitement. They're amped. You're trying to stay light. You're making jokes, playing the road trip playlist, trying not to go quiet. But suddenly, you start noticing the lyrics. Every song feels like it's aimed directly at you. Somehow, they all hit differently, like they were written just for this moment. That lump in your throat is growing. You're not crying. You're just focused. Right?

Arrival is chaos disguised as a system. There are student volunteers, rolling carts, key cards, check-in desks. Somehow, it works. You haul everything in. You get sweaty. You build the IKEA storage units. You rearrange the beds three times. You hang the curtains, the lights, and clip the small fan to the bed rail to keep the lofted bunk cool at night. You plug in the standing Vornado fan you made sure every kid had. It's the same hum they've always fallen asleep to at home, and you didn't want that to change.

Mom went full mom-mode. I had my toolkit. We both knew our jobs. Mom picked out the towels and bedding herself, because a pre-packed dorm bundle was not going to cut it. It took a while to arrange the room and assemble the furniture, but somehow it all came together. Amazing how much you can cram into a tiny space when you're emotionally unprepared to leave it.

Then you shift from building mode to background mode. You introduce yourself to the neighbors with a quick, 'Hi, we're the parents, this is our son or daughter, nice to meet you.' You hold the trash. You stand in the corner while they unbox their whole new life. You find yourself quietly watching them settle in, unsure if you're being helpful or just…there. You realize you're acting like everything's normal, because it kind of is. It's just new. And strange. And big.

Once we finished setting up our son, we went to lunch with his roommate and family. That's when it hit. The shift from decorating and doing to actually saying goodbye.

We recommended one last Target run, like parents trying to avoid the inevitable. Checked for toothpaste, tissues, snacks, anything to buy just to extend the time. But eventually, you hit that moment.

The final hug.

You stall. You ask one more time if they need anything. You say all the things you practiced. Be safe. Call us. We're proud of you. We love you.

You don't say: Please stay small just a little bit longer.

And then you shut the car door. They wave. You drive away. The car is quiet.

That was Iowa. Our first drop-off with our firstborn. The one that teaches you how hard this really is.

My wife remembers exactly where he stood as we pulled away. He looked… something. Maybe sad. Maybe alone. Maybe uncertain or scared or even a little excited but trying not to show it. We weren't sure. That's what made it harder. That image was frozen in her mind. For me, I tried to focus on how excited he was, how ready he seemed, the big opportunities ahead, the welcome events waiting and all the people he was about to meet. But I saw it too.

Some parents cry. Some don't. I held it together. My wife didn't. Neither was wrong. We were both exhausted, from packing, from emotion, and from the heartbreak that somehow arrived dressed as pride.

By the time we did it again 2 years later, we thought we'd be better at it.

At Alabama, there was a different kind of energy. Pure excitement, rush week chaos, and a campus that felt like a movie set. She was ready. We were proud. It was still hard. That goodbye hug on the sidewalk in front of the dorm felt just as heavy, only this time it came with heat, humidity, and the knowledge we couldn't drive back in a day if she needed us.

Then came Mizzou. The last drop-off. The car was packed to the roof, again. We'd done this twice before, but nothing prepares you for knowing it's the last time you'll unpack a dorm room. We stood there watching her make the bed, hang the photos, and laugh with her new roommate, realizing this was the end of an era. Every move, every Target run, every piece of advice had led to this moment. There was pride, and there was ache. Not just for who she'd become, but for the version of our family that existed before this day. The one where the everyday moments had built our life as a family under one roof.

**The Ride Home**

The drive home after college drop-off is like the emotional hangover you didn't prepare for. The adrenaline of the day has worn off. Your back hurts from moving bins, your muscles are cramping, your shirt is damp and sticking to you, and then it hits: you're driving home without your kid.

It's just you. Maybe your spouse. Maybe a long stretch of silence broken only by the occasional sniffle or sigh.

You thought the hard part was the goodbye in the dorm.

Turns out, it's pulling into your driveway without them. For us, that moment hit differently each time.

My wife broke first. She cried in the driveway. When we dropped off our son, the girls were still in high school, but saying goodbye to our firstborn hit hard. It happened again when we came home from dropping off our Mizzou daughter, only this time the house was officially empty. That's when I decided to take my wife to dinner, part comfort, part distraction. That dinner turned into a routine. For the next four years, we went out five or six nights a week. It was our version of coping, and honestly, it saved us.

It hit me once we were inside the house. I instinctively looked toward the dining room, still half expecting the move in piles to be there. The house was clean. Too clean. Too quiet. And don't get me started on walking past their bedrooms. When you do, it all hits you. Every time you stayed up with them when they were sick. Every school project spread out on the kitchen table. Every practice you drove to and every talk about doing the right thing.

You'll realize this is what it was all for. Raising them to be ready for this moment. Ready to leave. Ready to be okay without you right there.

And somehow, you'll survive it. Even if your heart forgets that for a minute.

You got them here. Now it's their turn to figure out what's next.

You'll feel everything. Excitement for them. Sadness for you. Fear. Pride. Wondering if they'll eat. If they'll make friends. If they'll remember to shower. They will. Eventually.

> **Mom's Take:** I thought I'd be fine. I'd already cried plenty in the weeks leading up to drop-off while packing his room, folding shirts, and watching him cross the high school graduation stage. But that final hug and the way he looked back one more time undid me. No matter how grown-up he seemed, all I could see was his kindergarten backpack on the very first day of school.
>
> With only our son away at school, I managed to hold it together a little easier because the girls were still home, filling the house with their schedules and everyday chatter. But when we came home from taking our Mizzou daughter and the house was officially empty, it was different. That quiet hit hard.

There's a strange emptiness in the house that first night. Not just the physical absence, but the absence of energy. No music coming from upstairs. No half-finished water bottles on the counter. No questions about what's for dinner.

And yet, you also realize... you're tired. The build-up to drop-off is intense. The last week at home is emotional. Move-in day is a full-contact sport. By the time you get home, you're drained. And maybe that's by design, so your emotions have space to land.

You'll check Find My iPhone. Maybe twice. You'll wonder if they're unpacking, if they met someone on their floor, if they had everything they needed.

And you'll debate texting. Should we check in? Or give space? We settled on this: in the beginning, it's natural to send a few hopeful texts. Keep them short, keep them light, and resist the urge to interrogate. Over time, you'll both figure out what works, but from day one, let them know the door (and phone line) is always open.

That ride home is your first lesson in letting go. You're not out of their life. You're just no longer in the front seat.

And that's okay. You've earned a nap. And maybe a drink and dinner.

They'll call. Probably for money. But hey, that still counts.

CHAPTER SIX

# Text Frequency and FaceTime Etiquette

Ah, the digital dance begins.

You're barely back home when it hits you. Should I text them? Are they okay? Did they eat? Do they even remember they have parents?

Spoiler: they do. They're just not sure how often they're supposed to respond. And let's be honest, neither are you.

Every family finds their rhythm. For us, it started with a few hopeful texts:

"How's the room?"

"Meet anyone yet?"

"Need anything?"

At first, the responses came quick.

"All good."

"Dorm's cool."

"About to head out."

Then came the silence.

You go from daily check-ins to radio silence faster than a freshman burns through dining dollars. Soon, you're staring at your phone, wondering whether your child fell off the grid or just got pulled into a free T-shirt giveaway and a dorm floor pizza party. It's almost always the latter.

After a few weeks into freshman year at Iowa, communication from our son basically went dark. Not a text, not a call, not even a random campus pic. My wife was checking his location at least twice a day like she worked in campus security. I finally caved and texted, "You good?" Five hours later he replied, "Yeah, just busy." That was it. Three words. No emoji. I guess we were expecting a novel and got a headline. We had apparently shifted phases from full-time parent to part-time subscriber.

Girls are a little different, but once college turns into its full-blown version of summer camp, they all end up in the same place: busy, happy, and impossible to reach. When our daughter first got to Bama, we heard from her constantly that first week. Photos of the dorm, texts about rush events, even updates on what she ate for breakfast. Then classes started and it all stopped. We went from daily play-by-plays to wondering if she'd joined a witness protection program. Turns out, she'd just joined a sorority. Same thing, different outfit.

Our daughter at Mizzou had a pattern. Every few weeks, I'd get a cheerful "Hi Dad!" text, which I quickly learned was code for "I'm about to ask for money." Sure enough, two messages later: "Any chance you could put money in my account to cover my groceries?" I didn't even mind. At that point, a text was a text.

Over time, we found our rhythm. Here's what worked *(and what didn't)*:

- **Don't panic.** They are not in danger. They are just distracted. Orientation events, roommate bonding, floor socials, and even the freshman tradition of building the giant "University Letter" on the football field for a photo op. You'll probably see that picture on Instagram before you even get a text back. Everything is loud, new, exciting, and a little overwhelming.
- **Let them initiate sometimes.** When they do, it's gold. That "What are the laundry instructions again?" text might make you tear up like you just won the Powerball but resist the urge to overdo it. Answer their question, give a quick tip, and let them feel like they figured it out.
- **Avoid the interrogation vibe.** Instead of "Where are you?" try "What's on deck today?" Mom had to fight her natural instinct to ask every follow-up under the sun. But she learned fast. Keep it light or risk total radio silence.
- **Accept the one-word replies.** Boys are champions of this. Our son once sent a photo of a sidewalk with sunshine and a single tree on campus. That was the update and somehow it said more than a full paragraph ever could. We took it.
- **FaceTime comes with rules.** Never randomly call or surprise them. Always send a heads-up text: "Hey, quick FaceTime?" If not, you might catch them mid-nap, mid-class, mid-meeting, or mid- "darty" *(that's day party, for the uninitiated).*
- **Group texts have potential.** Ours turned into a meme and inspirational quotes zone with the occasional "Check

your account" or "Send a pic from the game." It was low-pressure communication with high return.

> **Mom's Pro Tip:** Don't confuse silence for distance. They're busy building their own world, and that's exactly what you raised them to do. Stay calm, stay available, and trust that they'll reach out when it counts.

> **Dad's Pro Tip:** Keep your texts short and your expectations shorter. If you get a one-word reply, count it as progress. If you get a call, cancel your plans and enjoy the win.

From Mom's perspective, she talked to our son more on the phone than over text. She tried to keep it short, avoid being too nosy *(her words)*, and if he sounded distracted, she let him go. With our girls, she learned to ask fewer questions and give them space to come to her when they were ready. And they did. Eventually.

The unspoken truth? You miss them more than they miss you, at least right away. And that's a good thing. It means they're adjusting. It means they're okay. It means your parenting is showing.

But when they do call...

When they FaceTime out of nowhere...

When they text you a blurry photo of their breakfast pizza or the tailgate crowd or their decorated dorm door...

It's everything.

Because connection changes. It's no longer constant supervision.

It's subtle presence.

You're still there. Just in the background now.

And that's okay.

You raised them for this.

CHAPTER SEVEN

# Tailgating Without Embarrassing Them (Much)

This is where your second life as a college parent really begins. The dorm drop-off is behind you. The group chats have cooled off. And now it's fall, football season. And guess what? You're going back.

Tailgate season is where all your parenting, planning, and Pinterest-fueled outfitting comes full circle, with a side of BBQ, beer, and possibly one questionable decision involving Fireball.

We got a taste early. When our son initially considered Iowa, we visited on a game weekend and tagged along to a friend's tailgate. It was a blast. A preview of the party side of parenting. We looked at each other like, "So this is what we get to look forward to?"

What followed were tailgates at Iowa, Alabama, and Mizzou, each with their own flavor. Here's what we learned.

### Iowa: Midwestern Hospitality Meets Busch Light

You get there early. Like before-the-sun's-up early. You set up your spot with black and gold everything: tablecloth, plates, solo cups, bowls arranged next to the Hawkeye napkins and under the Hawkeye pop-up tent. Of course, there's the sonos speaker. We caved and bought ourselves one because relying on our son to bring his across campus was never going to happen more than once. And you pack enough layers to survive a Midwestern morning that starts at 40 degrees and ends in full sweat.

It's social and friendly. You're shaking hands with the family next to you, sharing breakfast sandwiches and drinks like you've known them since kindergarten. We brought the Cherry Bomb essentials in a cooler, poured and set them up to hand out like party favors. Our son's friends showed up hungry, and we were happy to feed them and their parents if they were visiting with no tailgate to attend. By the second visit, our son's friends were jumping in to help with setup and hauling coolers like part of the crew. It's the best. Also exhausting.

You have a few choices for the day. Get tickets and go to the game, stay and tailgate through it, or head to the bars to watch on TV. We've done all the above, and honestly, you can't go wrong. My wife might say she had more fun heading to Brother's or one of the other bars during the game. Just keep in mind, that option digs into your wallet even deeper than you've already invested in the weekend. Then again, depending on ticket prices, going to the game might be a wash or worse. The most budget-friendly move is to stay at your tailgate, enjoy what you brought, and hope someone nearby has a screen showing the game. You should still go to at least one though. "Back in Black" to start the game and the wave at the end of the first quarter are definitely worth experiencing.

Also, book your hotel rooms early. They aren't cheap on game weekends, and the best spots go fast. If you can't find something in town, check Coralville. It's easier on the budget and still has quick access to campus. Most every game weekend stay requires a two-night minimum. So, be prepared to drive in the night before. We always tried to get there Friday afternoon. It gave us time to hit the bookstore or Scheels for some gameday gear in advance, as if we didn't already have enough. It also gave us a chance to spend time with our son if he was free and not caught up in FAC, Friday Afternoon Club, at Airliner. The other bonus of arriving early is that Friday nights at the Ped Mall are alive with pre-game energy. You can catch the Hawkeye band marching from bar to bar playing fight songs while the crowd spills into the streets. And the food trucks? A grilled cheese and a gyro were always the perfect end to the night.

> **Dad's Pro Tip:** We bought a Coleman grill for the first season. Used it once. By the time we cooked, ate, packed, and cleaned it, the game was starting. We learned quick, stick to breakfast sandwiches, Casey's breakfast pizza, chili, deli meat, pulled pork sandwiches or anything that required less work. If you can eat it standing up with a drink in your hand, it's a win. The truth is, if you're the grill master, you miss out on the best part: the conversations, the laughter, and meeting people. Keep it simple and be present. That's what you'll remember.

**Bama: The Tailgate SEC-ond Coming**

You think you know tailgating? You don't. Not until Alabama. No cars on the Quad. You rent a tent. You cater the food. Parents roll in with hired bartenders and flatscreens powered by generators. Everyone is decked out in crimson and white. And there are rules. You only get three bins to bring in at 6 a.m. that volunteers will help you move, so you better plan accordingly. The rest? You're hauling it yourself. And good luck with parking. The streets are blocked off well before tailgating begins, which makes getting a car anywhere near the Quad almost impossible.

> **Pro tip:** We, along with our daughter's roommates' parents, stayed in our daughter's apartments we were already paying for. Not glamorous, but it saved a small fortune and was convenient.

Our first Bama tailgate? Total rookie move. We knew no one, didn't have a tailgate spot, and had zero experience securing one. So we wandered downtown Tuscaloosa with a drink in hand, watched the team buses roll through, listened as the crowd booed the visitors and cheered for the Tide, and wished we had an invite to one of those tents.

There are plenty of great spots near the stadium if you are not going to the game, but expect outrageous cover charges and long waits. With nearly 100,000 people in the stadium and even more outside it, getting into places can be tough. Rama Jama is one of the best historic stops, and the bucket of mimosas does not hurt either. Get there early on game day, or go another day and enjoy it.

Thankfully, we eventually figured out the Bama tailgating scene, thanks to the parents of our daughter's friend, who became good friends of ours. They had the process down, hosted a couple of tailgates, and eased us into the whole thing. By senior year, we finally felt comfortable enough to throw our hat in the ring and co-host one with the other families. By then, our daughter's apartment was just a short walk from Bryant-Denny and the Quad, which made the logistics much easier. Plus, we had learned the biggest hack of all: hotels and houses are ridiculously expensive on game weekends, so if you can crash at your kid's apartment, do it.

Before long, we were splitting a tailgate package with other families, catering food, and one of the dads proudly volunteered for Yellow Hammer duty, showing up with all the mixers like he was the honorary bartender of Tuscaloosa. Because down there, that drink is not optional. It's tradition.

My wife teamed up with the other moms, and the women basically ran point on setup. Once they had a group text going, it became a well-oiled machine with menus planned, supplies divided, and just enough crimson and white to mark our territory. We even mixed in a little black and gold since the game we co-hosted was Mizzou at Bama. Our Mizzou daughter and her friends came, and so did several of our parent friends from Missouri. It turned into the perfect crossover, parents from both schools we had been tailgating with for years finally sharing drinks, kids drifting between tents, and everyone swapping stories like old neighbors. What started as rookie wandering became a system. A community. And honestly, some of the best weekends of our lives.

> **Dad's Pro Tip:** Like most big football schools, visiting Bama wasn't cheap. Between airport parking, flights, rental car, hotel, food, drinks, and game tickets, each visit felt like a luxury vacation, only with more glitter, more rules, and way fewer nap opportunities. Restaurants also don't take reservations, so on game weekends, be ready to wait 3 to 4 hours for a table unless you show up at sunrise and put your name in.

**Mizzou: The Goldilocks of Tailgates**

Right in the middle. Geographically and vibe-wise. Mizzou gives you the SEC energy on a Big Ten budget. Tailgating there feels more like Iowa, familiar, festive, and still fully committed. You rent your spot in advance, drive in, unload, and build your black-and-gold zone like a seasoned pro. It's still crowded and still pricey, but manageable. The best part? You can walk to everything downtown afterward. Shots at The Shot Bar. Buzz Bombs at the Understudy. Rooftop fun at Heidelberg and Harpo's. Big crowds at Willie's and MyHouse. And the old staples like Campus Bar.

If you visit on Homecoming weekend, expect COMO to be bursting at the seams with alumni, fans, parents and game-day diehards ready to celebrate. The parade, the house skits, and the whole fall vibe make it one of the busiest times of the year on campus. Mizzou even lays claim to being the originators of Homecoming back in 1911, so it makes sense the celebration is a big deal (though Baylor and Illinois might argue otherwise).

We tailgated with families from home and picked up a few new ones along the way, because nothing builds friendships faster than sharing a cooler and a plate of tailgate food with the perfect party playlist blaring from the speaker. Our daughter was genuinely happy to see us. She was all in for dinner, tailgating, the game, and even drinks after. Our now-signature Cherry Bombs made the rounds again, which at this point probably deserve their own line item in the family budget.

> **Side Bar Moment:** If you ever have two kids in college whose teams face off, clear your calendar, you've got the makings of an epic family weekend. When Mizzou played at Bama, we threw a bash. Two daughters, two teams, and one tailgate full of school colors and southern humidity. Their friends, some of whom had only met over FaceTime, were now clinking Solo cups in real life and capturing the Instagram-worthy moments that would end up in their own highlight reel of college memories. It was the kind of chaotic, joy-filled crossover episode you don't plan... but never forget.

We had some truly epic tailgates over the years. There's nothing like waking up on a crisp Saturday morning, throwing on team colors, and knowing a full day and night of food, family, and fun is ahead. We had friends from home join us, family members who made the trip just to see what all the excitement was about, and many of our kids' friends from other colleges came to experience an Iowa, Mizzou or Bama weekend firsthand. Everyone tailgates a little differently, but that's part of the fun.

It's more than football. It's about connection, with siblings, grandparents, friends, and neighbors all becoming part of the weekend, part of the memory. Because in the end, tailgating isn't about where you are. It's about who you're with.

### The Tailgate Network

There's something about tailgating that turns strangers into instant friends. We'd show up, locate our spot, and within minutes someone from the next tent was handing us a plate of food or asking if we had a lighter. Before long, you're trading beers, swapping stories, and realizing you are all in this together. It's its own kind of parent fraternity, minus the pledge week.

By our second season, we started recognizing faces, figuring out who tailgated where, and learning the maps of each lot like it was our own neighborhood. You could always spot the veterans. They knew exactly which spots were gold. To get one, you must plan ahead and buy tailgate passes on Ticketmaster or StubHub, just like concert tickets. Most are being resold by people who already own the spots, and yes, that's a whole side hustle for the hardcore crowd. We learned to team up with other families to share the costs and the workload. It made the weekends more affordable, and a lot more fun.

> **Tailgate Pro Tip:** If you're grilling, plan your exit. You'll thank yourself later when it's kickoff time and you're staring at a hot grill, a half-empty cooler, and the sudden realization that everything you set up has to be torn down. Nothing humbles a parent faster than trying to collapse a pop-up tent after a few drinks and one bratwurst too many.

The grill can't go back in the vehicle until it's cooled off, so plan the shutoff in advance and see if anyone in your tailgate group wants to stay behind and keep the party going instead of heading to the game or the bar. Honestly, that happens a lot. Just know you'll still have cleanup duty when you get back, and probably a few new people hanging around your spot. That's the beauty of the tailgate community.

Tailgating can be a lot of planning and work. But the truth is, those weekends were some of the best times we've ever had. Laughing with other parents. Meeting our kids' friends. Feeling like we were part of something bigger. It wasn't just about football, it was about sharing a slice of their college world, together.

**A Few Universal Truths**

- **You will overspend.** On food, drinks, gear, parking, and hotel rooms with two-night minimums. And that's before the game tickets and more spirit wear for next time.
- **You will overpack.** Chairs, bags boards, extra coolers, a second speaker, backup batteries, way too much beer. Still not enough.
- **You will overdo it.** Especially if you try to hang like you're still in college. Don't be that parent. We've seen that parent. We've been that parent.
- **You will underprepare.** For the moment when your kid shows up at the tailgate, smiles, grabs a Cherry Bomb, and calls it "cool." For a parent, that is everything.

### Learn the Language

Every school has its own rally cry, and you'd better know how to respond. At Iowa, it's "Go Hawks." In Tuscaloosa, it's "Roll Tide." And at Mizzou, it's "M-I-Z…" with the expectation that you'll shout back "Z-O-U!" on cue. If you're wearing team colors anywhere, in town, in the stadium, even at the airport, these greetings are fair game. If someone calls one out, you answer. No hesitation. It's not just etiquette; it's membership in the club.

### Student Tickets: Worth Every Penny (and Sometimes a Profit)

One of our first lessons in college football parenting? Always buy the student ticket package for the season. Always.

At Iowa and Mizzou, it was simple. You could buy the full season up front. Alabama made it trickier, splitting the home schedule into "A" games and "B" games. If you wanted all of them, you had to get lucky or creative. By our daughter's junior year at Bama, she managed to score both A and B packages.

We bought them for each of our kids every year. Even if they didn't use every ticket, having them meant they could be part of the atmosphere anytime they wanted. And truth be told, student tickets are their own kind of currency. If they couldn't make a game, they could resell the ticket and turn it into fun money. And a Bama ticket for a sought-after game could be sold for a lot of fun money.

Our son never sold his. Not once. Even if he and his friends bailed at halftime to watch from a bar, he wanted to be there for "Back in Black" out of the tunnel and for kickoff, in the student section, right in the middle of it all.

Because sometimes the best part of game day isn't the game itself. It's just being there.

Tailgating is where the parenting shifts again. You're building community with your kid's friends, with other parents, and with your kid. It's bonding, just louder and stickier and five times more expensive.

And for a few hours, you're back in it. Music blasting. Grills fired up. Smell of fall in the air. Everyone in team colors, cheering for the same thing. You're not just visiting anymore.

You belong.

Just remember the ibuprofen. And maybe skip the third Fireball next time.

## CHAPTER EIGHT

# When You Visit — How to Be Wanted

Here's the golden rule of campus visits: don't overstay, overstep, or overpack your expectations.

You're stepping into their world now, not reliving your own glory days. Bring a good attitude, a few flexible plans, and your wallet open, but leave the emotional baggage at home.

### The First Visit

This one hits different. You're excited. They're… distracted. Maybe even acting like it's mildly inconvenient you're there.

They'll say things like, "You really don't have to come," but deep down, they're glad you did. Just don't expect a warm welcome committee. The vibe is: I'm happy to see you, but I'm also busy, I have plans, and I live here now.

For us, we learned to keep it simple. A dinner out. A Target run. A few minutes in the dorm to drop something off. That's it.

No long hangouts. No dramatic dorm move-in reenactments. No ambush photo shoots. Definitely no "We brought a few of your baby pictures to show your roommates" moments.

> **Mom's Take:** That first visit to Bama? We thought it would be the perfect chance to get the girls back together since they hadn't seen each other in person since move-in, only on FaceTime. Our Mizzou daughter made the trip down from Columbia with a few friends.
>
> But once we got there, our Bama daughter practically ghosted us all weekend. We got one dinner Friday night where she unloaded every highlight from her new life in one breath, rush week stories, game-day updates, roommate and sorority drama, and then she was gone, off to show her sister around and to meet friends. Tailgate plans the next day didn't include us either.
>
> So, we wandered the quad, watched the team buses roll through town, and tried to figure out what to do with ourselves. I was crushed at first. But I had to remind myself this was her finding her rhythm. By the next visit, we had both figured out how to meet in the middle.

### Know the Scene

Before you book the hotel, flight, or gas up the car, check the campus calendar and ask your kid what's happening that weekend. Parents Weekend, home game, Greek formals, sorority philanthropy events, homecoming, concerts, even career fairs can all send hotel rates up and keep your kid busy. Better to know if they're tied up with a "darty" before you roll into town.

If it's a game weekend, book early. And expect to be on your feet, on the move, and sometimes waiting around while they juggle you and their friends.

> **Dad's Pro Tip:** Hotels on game weekends will rob you blind. Depending on the school and the weekend, rooms can run anywhere from $500 to over $1,000 a night. One alternative is crashing at their apartment but be warned, it's a revolving door of friends at all hours. The kitchen that looked decent when we arrived was a sticky mess of spilled drinks, empty pizza boxes, and whatever late-night snacks came through the door by the end of the night. Fortunately, our daughter gave us her upstairs bedroom with a connected bathroom she actually cleaned in advance. It let us slip away on our own time, and with the fan humming, we could barely hear the chaos downstairs. We probably would not have done this at our son's place. Boys think "cleaning" means Febreze and shoving everything under the bed. The Febreze helps, but it still carries a faint undertone of beer and locker room that no candle or scented spray on earth can cover.

### Bring a Gift, Not a Guilt Trip

You're not there to lay into them for not calling. You're there to reconnect. A care package, a favorite snack, even some extra laundry detergent says, "I thought of you" without screaming, "I cried in your empty room last week." A team sweatshirt or t-shirt from the bookstore always lands too. They love that stuff.

**Dinners, Drinks, and Friend Time**

Offer to take them and a couple of friends out to eat. The key word here is "couple." Leave it vague and you will end up feeding a small village of 18-year-olds who will all politely offer to pay, knowing full well you are picking up the check anyway. Even if they did have their wallets, there is nothing in them. And honestly, you would not have it any other way.

Sometimes they'll linger. Sometimes they'll bail right after dinner. Either way, it's okay. Go explore the town, grab a drink, pop into the bookstore, sit on a bench near campus and soak it all in.

Being nearby matters more than you realize.

> **Mom's Take:** Our Mizzou daughter always made time for us. She loved the visits, tailgating, dinner, walking us through campus like a tour guide who knew the secret spots. Our Bama daughter? She mostly had her own itinerary, and we were lucky to get penciled in. She was much better about it by her Junior and Senior year. Each kid is different. Each visit is different. The best thing you can do is stay adaptable and try not to take it personally.

**Don't Overdo the Check-Ins**

One solid connection is worth more than hovering all weekend. Let them lead. If they want to show you everything, let them. If they want to keep it brief, go with it.

Remember, you're not the main character anymore. You're the

supporting cast. Proud, caffeinated, and occasionally swiping the parental credit card.

If they say they're tired? Believe them. If they say they've got plans later? Let them go.

A good visit should feel like a bonus, not a performance review.

**The Goodbye**

Before you even get to the hug, know this: parents and college kids are on different clocks. You are up early, already thinking about breakfast, a quick Target run, maybe one more meal together before hitting the road. They are still asleep. And honestly, they need it. Do not take it personally. Their late nights and jam-packed social schedules mean mornings are sacred. If you want that last Target run or brunch, communicate it ahead of time. Do not expect them to read your mind when all they can think about is ten more minutes of sleep.

So, when it is finally time to leave, hug them like you mean it. Don't linger. Don't guilt them into one more Target run. Just say, "Love you, proud of you," and let them walk away like the semi-adult they're becoming.

Then get back in the car, take a deep breath, and do your own little processing. You'll be back soon enough.

> **Dad's Take:** We didn't go to our son's very first game day at Iowa. We figured it was better for him to dive into the experience without having to play host to us. That afternoon, the university did a 360-degree panoramic crowd photo from the 50-yard line and posted a link so fans could zoom

in and find friends and family in the stands.

I searched for a while, but when I finally spotted him, dressed in black and gold with the biggest smile on his face, it hit me. I didn't recognize a single person around him. I didn't know if he was with friends or just caught up in the moment by himself. But there he was, happy, right in the middle of his new world.

I took a screenshot. I've looked at it a hundred times since. It made me proud, happy, and a little sad all at once. But mostly, it confirmed we'd made the right choice that day, giving him the space to live it on his own. That picture told me everything I needed to know.

### What Actually Makes a Visit "Good" (According to Our Kids)

We asked. They answered. Here's what stuck with them *(and what didn't).*

**The Wins**

- "Thanks for the Chick-fil-A and laundry pods."
- A spontaneous coffee run just the two of you.
- Letting them pick the dinner spot, even if it's not the cute place you found on Yelp.
- Bringing a sibling or friend for backup emotional energy.
- Keeping things short but showing up anyway.

**The Flops**

- Hovering too long in their dorm or apartment.
- Insisting on a photo around every corner.

- Posting unapproved photos of your visit on Instagram.
- Correcting or judging how they do things.
- Asking too many questions in front of their friends, or too many questions period. *("Do you still have that rash?" is never a good opener.)*

> **Parent Pro Tip:** If you leave behind a care package, gift cards, or a fresh roll of quarters for laundry, you will be remembered like a legend.

## CHAPTER NINE

# Meeting Their Friends (Without Being a Buzzkill)

At some point, probably over a plate of tailgate nachos or a casual drink downtown, you'll meet the friends. These are the kids your son or daughter has been texting, posting with, or casually referencing by first name only, as if you should already know who they are.

This is a critical parenting tightrope walk. You want to be warm but not weird. Interested but not invasive. Fun but not trying too hard.

We've both been there, hovering a little too long after dinner or asking one too many follow-ups that instantly kill the vibe.

Here's what we've learned about doing it right:

**Rule #1: Be Cool**

That doesn't mean squeezing into skinny jeans or rocking the latest sneakers like you're trying to rush, midlife edition.

It means this:

Don't interrogate. Don't lead with, "So, do you guys go out a lot?" Definitely don't try to relate by referencing your own college stories unless they specifically ask.

Smile. Shake hands. Say something casual about their school gear or how cold it's gotten this week. Then back off and let them come to you. Of course, where are you from, what made you choose the university and what are you studying are always "go-to" starters.

> **Mom's Take:** The first time I met our son's roommate crew, they were definitely trying to gauge what kind of mom I was. "Is she going to be cringey? Ask too many questions? Try to follow us on Instagram?" I smiled, said hi, asked about their majors, then just listened. One of them offered to help carry our cooler, and suddenly we were laughing together like we'd known each other for a while. With guys, it is simple: do not overthink it, do not overshare. Just be present and chill. Desperation? They can smell it.

**Rule #2: Pick Up the Tab**

This is the easiest win in the book. If you are taking them out for coffee, dinner, or drinks, just cover it. Quietly. No announcement. No expectation. It is not about flexing. It is about creating space for connection.

Some of our best moments with our kids' friends came not from planned bonding but from just showing up and sharing a table. You would be surprised how quickly they open up when food is involved and the vibe is low pressure.

> **Dad's Note:** They'll thank you, almost always. We always found the students to be super polite. A lot of our kids' friends would ask for our numbers just to send a follow-up thank you. That kind of thoughtfulness? Totally unexpected but really appreciated.

**Rule #3: Know When to Exit**

If the conversation starts shifting into "what's next tonight," that's your cue. Don't overstay the invite. You're not here to be their new best friend. You're just the well-dressed guest who brought the energy, picked up the tab, and left before things got weird.

If they say, "You should come with us," great. Smile and appreciate it. In the early years, we tagged along, and it was fun seeing our kids in their element. Just remember, the bars are loud, conversations are impossible, and every step feels like you're walking on duct tape. Then comes the question: pay for the round or start a tab? Early on, you'll start the tab. Then you learn. Those tabs run up fast, and if you stay long enough, they're always bigger than you expected, even for a college bar. Over time, we started limiting our late-night college bar time, partly age, partly wisdom. My wife's more of a night owl, I'm more of a day drinker, so we found a rhythm. Sometimes we'd hang for a bit, then let them move on to the next bar while we ducked out. Many nights we found a quiet spot for a nightcap, a place where we could actually hear each other and relive the day in peace.

However, sometimes the cooler move is to skip the bar scene. Leave on a high note, keep your "fun parent" status intact, and make the next visit feel like something they actually look forward to.

> **Mom's Take:** I always wondered if my daughters' friends would like me. But when I met them, I just treated them like I'd known them forever. Asked questions, listened, smiled. Nothing over the top. I was genuinely interested in who they were. And that seemed to matter. They'd hang out at our tailgate, start real conversations, and more often than not, we'd follow each other on Instagram and text afterward. Turns out, being warm and curious, without turning it into a performance, goes a long way.

> **Bonus Tip: Don't Try to Be the "Fun Parent":** You can absolutely be fun. Take the group to a game, host a tailgate, even take a round of shots if it feels right. But don't try to match their energy shot-for-shot or get pulled into a 1 a.m. bar crawl if you've been up since 5 a.m. setting up the tailgate. You are not in college. You are financing college.

> **Dad's Reminder:** I've seen parents get a little too caught up in the fun. My own wife once hit the floor at a rooftop bar during a Mizzou tailgate weekend. She blamed the shoes. I gently helped her up and said, "Time to call it a night." You don't need to keep up with the college crowd. Just show up, enjoy it, and know when to tap out.

**The Real Goal**

You're not trying to win over their friends. You're trying to show your kid you trust them. That you're here to support, not embarrass. That you can be part of their world without taking it over.

A little effort goes a long way.

A little space goes even further.

And years later, when their friends still say, "Your parents are the best," you'll know you struck the balance just right.

CHAPTER TEN

# Welcome to Greek Life – Bring Your Wallet

Just when you thought you'd mastered dorm life and FaceTime boundaries, a new chapter begins. One with chants, special handshakes, choreographed dances, and invoices.

Welcome to Greek Life, where friendships are forged, t-shirts multiply like rabbits, and your bank account slowly waves goodbye.

Let's start with the basics. All three of our kids joined Greek life: our son at Iowa, and our daughters at Mizzou and Alabama. That's Phi Kappa Psi, Gamma Phi Beta, and Zeta Tau Alpha, respectively. I now own more "Dad's Weekend" shirts than regular shirts, and apparently they are all considered vintage the minute the weekend is over.

But let's be clear: the initiation into Greek life starts long before they're officially in. It begins with quiet conversations like "Are you rushing?" that quickly escalate into full-blown wardrobes, headshots, and curated social feeds. Especially at Alabama, where Rush isn't just a week. It's basically a reality show via TikTok. There were outfit checklists, consultants, daily breakdowns of which houses were still in play, and more emotional swings than a season of The Bachelor. Our daughter handled it with grace, but it was a lot. For everyone.

Once they're in, it's like joining a country club you're not allowed to visit, but you definitely still have to pay for.

**Sorority Life: Glamorous… and Expensive**

Let's start with the girls. If you have daughters, know this: sorority dues don't just cover T-shirts and glitter. They include meals, which you pay for whether they eat them or not, chapter fees, social events, philanthropy projects, formals, and endless spirit gear. And just when you think you're caught up, another Venmo request lands, or a surprise line item on some random invoice. It feels like invoices are flying at you from every direction, each hidden behind a different portal with its own login. Honestly, I'm half convinced they don't consolidate them on purpose, so you'll miss one, rack up a late fee, and pay even more.

Zeta at Alabama was on another level. The house was stunning. Southern Living magazine meets high-end event space. Full-time chefs, gorgeous lounges, manicured everything, fresh flowers everywhere. It was a place you'd feel lucky just to tour, let alone live in. But yes, the cost reflected that. Even if our daughter was not living in the house, the meal plan was mandatory, so you paid for it whether she ate there or not.

Mizzou was more low-key but still packed a financial punch. Our daughter lived in the Gamma Phi house for a year, which helped consolidate rent and meals, but with every philanthropy event, sisterhood night, and sweatshirt drop, it felt like our bank account was pledging right alongside her.

Eventually we stopped keeping track of what was "extra" and just filed everything under college expenses. Tuition. Books. And sorority hoodies.

> **Mom's Take:** Rush Week was a whole production. We weren't just shopping, we were curating outfits like it was the Met Gala on a Target budget. I worried about the pressure she felt to "be the right version of herself," but I also saw her confidence bloom. That first sorority selfie? She looked like she belonged, and she knew it.

### Fraternity Life: Slightly Less Formal, Still Expensive

Our son joined Phi Psi during his sophomore year at Iowa. He didn't live in the house, but he found his people there. Guys who shared his values, pushed him to stay focused, and gave him the kind of community every parent hopes their kid finds in college.

That fraternity gave him structure, real friendships, and, let's be honest, some much-needed accountability. He had to keep his grades up, and he did. There were organized study hours, people to lean on academically, and a sense of responsibility that seemed to click for him.

Of course, it wasn't all quiet growth and group chats. He also participated in their early morning game-day tradition: a 5 a.m.

walk to the fraternity house to shotgun a beer before heading home to rest up before the actual tailgate started. College logic at its finest.

Less glitter, more Solo cups. But the monthly costs to belong and actually participate kept coming.

Still, even with the dues and occasional expenses, the experience was worth it. He didn't just join a fraternity. He found his footing.

**Hidden Costs and Pro Tips**

**1. The Apparel Avalanche**

There will be more Greek-lettered clothing than laundry days. Spirit jerseys, tanks, big/little reveal hoodies, party shirts. Some are adorable. Some get worn once. All are mysteriously essential.

**2. The Social Scene Drain**

If your kid is social, and most of them are once they join a house, just accept the ongoing expenses: Ubers, meals out, clothes for theme parties, and occasional weekend getaways for formals or spring events. Plan accordingly. And maybe don't check the Venmo feed too often.

**3. The Emotional ROI (Return on Investment)**

This is where it all starts to feel worth it. These are the people they'll do life with. The ones who help carry them through roommate drama, exams, and real-world fears. We watched our daughters grow stronger, more confident, more rooted. And our son found his crew too. Guys he could trust, rely on, and make memories with that didn't involve us constantly hovering nearby.

We didn't always get to see them as much as we wanted when we visited, especially early on when everything was new and they were figuring it out. But we knew they were making connections, building their people, and starting to thrive.

Would we do it again? Absolutely.

Would we budget better next time? Without a doubt.

Would we ever understand how they have more Greek gear than actual clean laundry? Not in this lifetime.

But for everything it gave them, and taught us, we'd set up auto-pay and do it all again.

CHAPTER ELEVEN

# Lease Season and Apartment Scouting

It'll happen earlier than you think:

"Hey, I need to start looking at places for next year."

Wait, what? Didn't you just get there?

Welcome to lease season, which at most schools, starts well before you're emotionally or financially ready. Just when you're settling into your new rhythm at home and mastering the art of not checking Life360 every ten minutes, they're ready to talk floorplans, rent, and roommate combos.

## The Timeline Shock

By October of freshman year, many students are already locking in roommates and signing leases for the following fall. It feels ridiculous, but it's real. The good spots near campus go fast. So yes, you might be Christmas shopping and apartment hunting at the same time. The good news is, they typically do this part on their own. The first big adulting move. Of course, that's easy to do when there is no financial obligation on their end.

The first time it happened, we were stunned. Our son casually brought it up like he was asking for more toothpaste: "I think we're signing a lease this week." He was still figuring out his classes and hadn't mastered laundry yet, but he was suddenly ready to lock down rent and roommates ten months out.

### Who They Live With Matters More Than Where

Freshman-year roommate frustrations are common. Some kids get lucky. Others, not so much. Our son's first roommate left just two days into the semester due to illness. His next assigned roommate wasn't exactly a great fit, and within days, he called home ready to pack it up. We told him gently but firmly that coming home wasn't an option. What was an option? Figuring it out. And to his credit, he did.

He found a loophole and heard about another guy in his dorm who was in a similar situation. One knock on the kid's door and five minutes of conversation later, they had swapped roommates and moved in together. That final hour switch turned into a great friendship and a two-year apartment roommate for sophomore and junior years that worked. They are still good friends today.

And the full-circle moment? His original roommate, the one who went home due to illness before freshmen year started, ended up living with him again senior year, after the rest of the roommates had moved on. They reconnected like no time had passed. A year or two after graduation, our son stood beside him at his wedding as his best man. Proof that sometimes, the best parts of college aren't planned, they're figured out.

The lesson? Let them take the lead, but push for real conversations upfront: cleaning habits, overnight guests, who's buying the toilet paper, and how the bills get split. More than one friendship has been wrecked over an unpaid water bill and a sink full of soggy cereal bowls.

**Location, Location... and Laundry**

Being close to campus is gold, especially during that first year which is normally a dorm anyway. Walkability matters. No need for a car, a parking pass, or figuring out a bus schedule to get to class. You want them focused on figuring out their independence, not navigating cross-town logistics just to make it to a lecture.

Most students make the move to an apartment by sophomore year, unless they're living in a fraternity or sorority house. And once that apartment life begins, so does the era of repeat moves, lease overlaps, sublets, and storage puzzles. Doesn't matter how far away the new place is, every move is its own operation. And you're almost always involved.

If the apartment isn't furnished, get ready to source and ship beds, couches, and whatever IKEA storage unit they saw on TikTok. Moving day gets a lot less fun when you're the one carrying the drawers up three flights of stairs because the elevator's broken and the AC isn't turned on yet. And typically, August is the month for moving, often one of the hottest months of the year.

And somehow, you always show up, toolbox in hand, pretending this will be the last one.

**Dad Sidebar: Nailed It. Literally.** By senior year, you think you've earned a break. The final apartment. The final move. The final IKEA bed assembly. I had even started giving myself little pats on the back, like look at me, still showing up with tools and optimism.

Our Mizzou daughter had landed in her seventh college housing situation (yes, seventh), but this one felt like a win. Nicer place, the upper classmen side of town, cheaper rent, and she was sharing it with three friends. We'd already helped her move in. Dresser builds? Check. Flatscreen hung? Complete. Bed frames? Done.

Then, one month later, we drove back for a football weekend. Our daughter had printed a few posters and asked if I'd hang them. Naturally, that's Dad Duty. I'm the guy with the toolkit and the "eye for balance." After a nearly six-hour drive, I just wanted to knock them out before we checked into the hotel and kicked off the weekend.

The first four went up like a dream. The fifth? That one will go down in college move in history.

The lease had a clause forbidding command strips, which I usually use, so I went old school with nails. The stud finder said I was good. I tapped it in. A little resistance. Hmm. Weird feel. I pulled the nail back out. Boom. Drywall shrapnel to the face and the sound of a freight train hissing behind the wall.

I'd hit the copper line connected to the AC compressor. Freon was shooting out like it was trying to escape the lease too.

I did what any former construction kid would do: plugged the hole with my finger and yelled for my daughter to call maintenance. The guy who showed up? Son of the landlord, mid-20s, dressed for a golf tee time. Needless to say, his Friday plans were shot too.

Three days without AC, 80+ degree heat, one ruined wall, and a deposit we'll never see again. But hey, memories, right? All I wanted was to hang the frames and head to Logboat Brewery. Instead, I got a crash course in HVAC systems and an unintentional comedy show.

Moral of the story? Even seasoned DIY dads can take down an AC unit. Read the lease, respect the drywall, and maybe still pack the Command Strips. Just in case.

**Mom's Take:** My job during move-in? Scrub every inch of that place like I was prepping it for an open house. Floors, baseboards, fridge, oven, bathroom, if it could hold bacteria, I was on my hands and knees with a disinfectant. My husband would walk in, look around at the empty walls and freshly painted rooms, and say, "Looks clean to me." But moms have bionic eyes. We see dirt from space.

I pretended to hate it, but honestly, I liked knowing they were starting fresh. I gave my standard lecture on keeping it clean. The girls got it. My son just nodded like he was listening, but his eyes said, "None of this is landing." And it didn't. But I cleaned it anyway.

### Budget Talk (Again)

Apartments come with a new layer of budgeting: rent, utilities, internet, trash, water, parking. Some places look affordable until you realize nothing is included and the "amenities fee" means you're paying $60 a month to walk past the barricades next to the pool that's under construction.

Sit down and go over what's covered, what's not, and who's paying for what. We always encouraged ours to get a part-time job if their schedule allowed. Not to cover the essentials; we handled rent, groceries, and utilities, but for spending money. It made a difference. Once it was their own money on the line, those weeknight outings suddenly became a lot less frequent.

> **Dad's Pro Tip:** If you've ever moved furniture in 100-degree heat after a moving company fumbles your reservation, you've earned the right to veto any unfurnished apartment moving forward. Bonus points if your kid learns what a hex key is, the tiny L-shaped tool responsible for the permanent callus on my hand.

> **Pro tip within a Pro Tip:** If you're driving instead of flying, bring a drill with hex bits or a Swiss Army knife of Allen wrenches. Your hands and your sanity will thank you.

### Watch for Scams & Pressure

College towns can be a wild west of leases. Landlords know they have leverage, and students can get swept up in the panic. "This place will be gone by tomorrow!" is a popular scare tactic.

Some of them will sign just to avoid FOMO.

Help them slow down. Read the lease. Better yet, have someone else review it too. Although we didn't utilize it, many schools have legal aid or student resources that can help with lease reviews. It's worth the extra step. Some leases are loaded with fine print, confusing fees, or policies that don't show up until move-in day. Better to catch it early than be surprised later.

And yes, your name is probably going on that lease. Unless your kid has income and credit, they will need a guarantor. That's where you come in. You won't be on the lease as a tenant, but your name will be the safety net. Make sure you know what you're guaranteeing and read the fine print before signing anything.

> **Parent Reminder:** Don't wait until move-in week to buy the essentials. Target, Amazon, IKEA, they all get picked over fast in college towns. We learned the hard way that storage bins, fans, throw rugs, and organizers basically vanish in those stores by the time you arrive. Ship what you can ahead of time, or shop early while it's still in stock.

Bottom line? Apartment hunting is one of their first real adult moves. Let them take the reins but stay close enough to spot the potholes. Ask questions. Offer calm. Double-check the lease.

Because once the lease is signed, guess who's showing up with the moving truck, an Allen wrench, and questionable decision-making energy? You.

**Mom's Pro Tip:** Expect shared costs for kitchens and shared bathrooms, but when possible, choose furnished apartments, especially if they'll be there for a few years. No moving. Much simpler furniture logistics. Unfurnished places can work, just know you'll be sharing the cost of couches, TVs, stools, décor, and more, along with the fun of delivery, assembly and setup. And when it's time to move out, everything has to be sold, divided, or hauled away. Our girls sold most of it on Marketplace and split the money, at a much lower value, of course. If you don't sell it, cue the moving truck again. And trust me, after a few big spills, most of that furniture isn't worth keeping anyway.

## CHAPTER TWELVE

# Moving Mayhem — Dorms to Apartments

The myth of the "One Big Move".

You think there's one big college move, the freshman drop-off, and you're done. Cute.

The truth? Moving is not a one-time event. It is a recurring nightmare (or adventure, depending on the day) that happens every year, every lease change, every internship, and every graduation. And if you have multiple kids in college, welcome to the College Parent Logistics Olympics.

We were basically in constant motion. Dorms, apartments, summer storage, even post-grad moves to new cities. Moving trucks had a way of disappearing right when we needed them most, but one saint of a rental clerk came through and saved my soul.

### Round One: The First Dorm Move

Our son was our guinea pig for our inaugural move-in day. Iowa City was two and a half hours from home, close enough for a day trip but far enough to feel like the start of something big.

We fit everything into the rental as planned. The futon we ordered through the university was being delivered straight to the dorm room. That was the easy part. Putting it together, even after watching the YouTube video step by step, in a two-person dorm room with barely enough space to blink, let alone maneuver, may have been the most physically difficult and frustrating part of the entire move. At one point, it felt like the futon and I were wrestling for dominance. Worth it, though. That thing moved out of Iowa City and eventually landed in Columbia, Missouri, living in at least three different apartments that I know of. Honestly, I wouldn't be surprised if it's still out there today, supporting some sophomore who has no idea it once broke a grown man's spirit.

This move spoiled us. Every move after this one felt like pure chaos.

And just when we thought we had it down, the world threw a plot twist.

Sometimes things happen you cannot see coming.

### When COVID Hit

Seven months after that first move in, the world shut down. The dorms that had been buzzing with new friendships and Friday night energy were suddenly being emptied. During the move-out, everyone wore masks. Parents and kids packed in near silence, glancing at each other like, “What is happening?”

We borrowed a trailer from a friend and hauled everything we had just moved in right back home. There were no goodbyes this time. Just eerie silence, scheduled moveouts, rushed packing, and a feeling that none of us knew what was really happening. We drove home that day in a daze.

Our son finished the rest of his freshman year online from home. And while we were grateful to have him back under our roof, something had shifted. All the emotions we felt the first time we let him go, the anxiety, the uncertainty, the ache, came rushing back, but in a different way. Not because we had to say goodbye again, but because we could already see how much he had grown in such a short time.

He needed space. He needed independence. And even though we loved having him home, we could tell that school, that campus, that community, that life, had become his happy place. It was the first real glimpse of what the rest of his life might look like. He was becoming who he was meant to be, and all we could hope was that the world would eventually get back to normal so he could get back to it.

That fall, he moved back. This time into an off-campus apartment we had already signed for months earlier. That move was mask heavy too. Hot August weather. Long elevator lines. And the surreal sense that college life had completely changed. He managed classes online from that apartment for the first semester, until campus finally reopened for in person learning and things slowly started to feel normal again.

**Enter the Twins: Double the Colleges, Triple the Chaos**

Two years later it was time for moves to Mizzou and Alabama.

Alabama move in was first and turned into a total logistical scramble. We were moving our daughter and two of her roommates together since all three were from northern Illinois. The plan was to reserve a truck large enough to fit everything for all three girls. We would take each of the girls' belongings to the home of the family who would be driving the truck. The dad would make the drive south, and the rest of us would either fly or drive down separately.

The truck was supposed to be picked up and loaded the day before the drive. There was just one problem: it didn't exist. The online reservation was confirmed, but no truck was waiting in person. What followed was a mad dash to find another one at a time when nearly everything was already booked. Thankfully, the dad found one, got it loaded, and made the drive to Tuscaloosa.

The university does not allow moving trucks on campus, so we got creative. The contents of the truck were unloaded into the basement of our Airbnb, which thankfully had an exterior door right next to the driveway for easy access. Each girl had a different move-in time, so we rented a 15-passenger van and removed the seats. One by one, we transferred their things from the Airbnb to campus and got them moved in.

Our daughter's move-in time was last, but the parents ahead of us graciously moved in some of the shared items along with her larger pieces when it was their turn. It was thoughtful, and very much appreciated.

One week later we did it again at Mizzou. Another moving

company fail. The pull behind trailer we reserved was nowhere to be found. The company came through and "upgraded" us to a 15-foot box truck for only $20 to make up for the inconvenience. A great deal, except we had to drive that beast six hours each way. Of course, our daughter rode in the comfortable car with her friends who were taking their cars down for freshman year.

> **Dad's Pro Tip:** Be careful trusting online reservations for moving trucks. The corporate site will happily take your booking, but it doesn't always know what the local or satellite location actually has in stock. Even if you call to confirm, things can fall through. Always have a backup plan or know another rental company nearby, just in case you're met with the dreaded "we don't have that truck" surprise.

> **Mom's Pro Tip:** If your kid stays over the summer for residency or work, factor in extra moves. A short-term sublease might sound simple, but it usually means more hauling between dorms, summer apartments, and permanent housing in the fall.

### The Sophomore Shuffle: Apartments and Sorority Houses

Just when we thought we had freshman moves figured out, sophomore year brought a new twist: off campus living and Greek life.

For our daughter at Alabama, moving out of the dorm and into her first apartment should have been easier. It wasn't. The Zeta house is huge, but didn't have enough rooms for her entire pledge class. She volunteered to live off campus, which was what she wanted anyway, so we shifted gears and started prepping for apartment life instead of sorority living.

We avoided summer storage fees by moving most of her belongings into a sorority sister's apartment that sat empty for the summer. The rest we loaded into a moving trailer and hauled back to Illinois. It sounded simple, but turned into a puzzle of coordinating schedules, key handoffs, and figuring out what to leave behind versus what to bring home.

When she returned in the fall, she drove her own car down for the first time, which helped. She had sorority duty and stayed in the house for two weeks to prep and work rush week. Her car was packed full of clothes and essentials from home, while we flew down and rented a larger vehicle to move the bigger items from the sorority sister's apartment into her new place.

The logistics worked, but the Tuscaloosa heat and sheer volume of stuff made it feel like a full-blown endurance event.

> **Dad's Pro Tip:** At Alabama, even if your daughter lives off campus, you may still be paying for the sorority house meal plan. We paid full rent on an apartment and still got charged for meals at the house. She ate there most every day, so it wasn't wasted, but in hindsight, we would have saved money by having her live in the house. It might not be their first choice, but it could be the smarter one for your wallet.

Our daughter at Mizzou chose to stay on campus over the summer after freshman year to earn Missouri residency, so the logistics for her sophomore year started early. Instead of coming home, we moved her out of the dorm and into a small apartment she subleased for the summer. It was bare bones, but furnished and served its purpose. A place to sleep and store her things while she worked and took classes.

By fall, she moved again into her sorority house. This time there were no challenges. Her bigger items were already stored in the basement of the house from the spring move out. She had worked hard during her freshman year to earn enough points, a mix of grades, involvement, and participation, to place high on the room selection list. That effort paid off. She was able to choose a three-bedroom space for herself and the two friends she had planned to live with. The house was beautiful and felt like a reward for how much she had invested to get there.

### The Sweet Lady at the Moving Company (a.k.a. My Favorite Stranger)

By junior year, our daughter at Alabama was moving again, this time into a complex closer to Bryant Denny. Eleven of her sorority sisters plus her were moving into a small two-building setup with a shared courtyard in between. For them, it sounded like a dream. For the parents, another logistical workout.

The challenge was timing. Her old lease ended two days before the new one started. Everything had to be loaded into a moving van or truck, sit at our hotel for two nights, and then be unloaded into the new place. We were seasoned at this point, practically professional movers, but this one tested every ounce of patience we had.

I rented the cargo van online, double-checked the reservation more times than I'd like to admit, and even called two days before our flight to confirm. That's when I learned there were no vans, no trucks, and even if there had been, the location would be closed the day we arrived. No staff. No access. No van.

The woman on the other end of the line was unbelievably kind. I took a deep breath and calmly explained our situation with flights booked and a rental car reserved and nowhere to store everything if we didn't have a van. She must have heard the desperation in my voice, the sound of a dad already defeated, and promised to make some calls to see what she could do. Somehow, she pulled it off. She called back and gave me step-by-step instructions on how to retrieve the keys from a lockbox, sign in through the app, and pick up the truck. I breathed a sigh of relief but stayed skeptical, right up until the moment we were actually sitting behind the wheel.

When we landed, the car we'd reserved was gone and the only option left was a Tesla. We had no idea if Tuscaloosa even had charging stations or how to charge one, which was just another worry added to the pile. By the time we reached the rental facility for the van, the usual paperwork had to be done entirely through my phone in front of a security camera in heat well over 100 degrees. My Maui Jim readers were useless in the blinding sun, sweat was stinging my eyes, and I looked like a confused street performer swiping at a mirror instead of a screen. The woman who helped us earlier finally called after watching me fumble on the security camera, and with her coaching I ditched Chrome for Safari, finished the process, punched in the lockbox code, and got the keys. Victory, but at the cost of dry clothes, my dignity, and at least a pint of sweat.

The move itself was brutal. By the time we finally reached her apartment with the van, the sun was already going down. The temperature had only dropped a few degrees, but without the sun beating down it was manageable. No change of clothes necessary. We decided it was best to push through and empty the apartment into the van that night, and worry about sleep later. It was the right call. The next day hit over 100 degrees again, and so did every day we were there. That's August in Tuscaloosa. No wonder they hand out mini battery-operated fans during rush week.

Two days later, we were at it again, this time unloading the van into the new apartment. Three flights of stairs, her bedroom on the second floor, and not a single piece of furniture in the place. We and the other three sets of parents had coordinated deliveries from IKEA, Target, Amazon and Ashley Furniture. Some parents made the trek by SUV or truck, which meant they could haul in the bigger shared items, something we were very grateful for.

The next two days were spent assembling furniture, hauling boxes, and turning bare apartments into homes. By the end of it, I am convinced I lost ten pounds in sweat and gained lifelong friendships with the other parents who were right there in the trenches with us.

When it was finally done, we returned the van and I met the woman in person who had saved us. I thanked her again. She hadn't just saved the move; she'd saved my sanity.

> **Dad's Pro Tip:** Check lease dates early. It is common for one lease to end a few days before the next one starts. Those gaps can turn you into a storage unit on wheels. If that happens, plan safe parking, locks, and what essentials your kid will need during the downtime.

**Moving Never Really Ends**

You think the last move will be graduation. It won't.

There will be first jobs, new cities, post grad apartments. You will sell cars, ship furniture, pack trailers, and say a hundred goodbyes. Each one will feel different. Less frantic, more bittersweet.

Moving is not just about the stuff. It is about seasons. Every load you carry is a reminder that they are growing up, and you are too.

If you're lucky, by the time you've packed your last IKEA bag, you'll know how to laugh when the truck doesn't show. Because it probably won't. And somehow, that'll be okay.

> **Dad's Pro Tip:** Remember that shared Google essentials list that somehow quadrupled? Every year you'll swear you'll bring less, and every year you'll toss half of it at move-out. Daughters, especially, seem to shed décor and storage pieces like last season's fashion. After graduation, our Mizzou daughter fit everything into her car, hard to believe it took a full moving truck just to get her there.

## CHAPTER THIRTEEN

# Scholarships, Financial Aid and "Can I Get More Money?"

Despite our best efforts, none of our kids snagged the mythical full-ride. No fancy checks at award night. Just FAFSA, loans, and the inevitable "Can I get more money?" text. Some families win the scholarship lottery. We didn't, so our talks were about loans, limits, and how to say no without guilt.

Our kids took the federal loans they qualified for, and we covered the rest. Not because we had a perfect financial plan, but because we wanted them to have some skin in the game without sinking under it. Was it ideal? No. But it was the deal we made, and like a lot of families, we made it work with a blend of budgeting, sacrifice, 529, Venmo, and crossed fingers.

Some months, that meant dialing back on extras. Some years, that meant postponing other plans. We knew our kids wouldn't graduate debt-free, but we could teach them how to manage the weight of their loans with eyes open and priorities straight.

> **Mom's Take:** I was usually the one who said yes. If they wanted to go on a trip, buy the dress, or join the fun, I didn't want them to miss out, especially if I could swing it. My husband handled more of the actual bills, and he'd give me the look. You know the one. But I always thought: they're working hard, college is short, and these moments matter. Did I say yes too often? Maybe. But I don't regret wanting to say yes when I could.

**When to Say No (or Not Yet)**

It starts innocently enough with the occasional "Can I…" text.

"Can I study abroad?"

"Can I go to Cabo for spring break?"

"Can I get concert tickets for one of my favorite artists coming to town?

"Can I move into that luxury apartment with the rooftop pool and wine fridge?"

> **Parent Reminder:** If it shows up as a Venmo request, it is probably a want. If they actually call you first, it might be a need. Nine times out of ten, it's still a want.

And suddenly, you're not just the parent, you're the bank manager, the risk analyst, and the CFO of their college lifestyle.

It's okay, more than okay, to say no. Or not yet. Or: "Sure, if you're paying for it."

The important part is being clear about what you're willing to cover, and what needs to come from their own hustle. These are the kinds of boundaries that help them grow up, even if they don't thank you for it until much later. If ever.

We tried to be consistent. We paid for the things we agreed to like tuition, rent, groceries, phone, a share of the gas. The rest? That was on them. And once they started working part-time or budgeting their own spending, something shifted. They made smarter choices. They weighed wants vs. needs. A $16 bar tab felt very different when it came out of their own account.

**Know the Loan Lingo**

There's no way around it, loans are a big part of most college journeys. And while you can't always change the cost, you can make sure your kid understands what they're signing.

Subsidized loans mean the government covers the interest while they're in school. Unsubsidized means the meter's running from day one. Neither is free money. It's a delayed bill with real consequences.

We made it a point to walk through the terms together. Not as a lecture, but as a lesson. Because even if they zone out halfway through the interest explanation, they need to know that repayment isn't optional and that debt doesn't magically disappear just because graduation comes with champagne and a diploma.

We didn't want them leaving college blind to what they owed. We wanted them to understand the weight of it without being crushed by it.

> **Dad's Pro Tip:** If you have access to their bank account, and you should, check it before responding to any "I need money for food" text. Nine times out of ten, the real story is in the transaction history. I had access because I was the one reimbursing them for items we agreed to cover. That made it easy to check, add things up, and pay them back.

### The Money Talk Is Never Just One Talk

It's a conversation that evolves semester by semester, as their needs shift and their independence grows.

We kept it honest. We didn't sugarcoat costs. And we didn't make money a taboo topic. If anything, we used those "Can I get more money?" texts as chances to talk about budgeting, priorities, and long-term impact.

And no, Cabo was never happening on our dime. She went anyway. When the group she traveled with ended up at Nobu for dinner and started wining and dining, she took one look at the menu and decided a single drink was all her budget could handle. My wife felt bad when she told us about it later. You want to swoop in and cover it so they do not feel left out, but part of growing up is realizing money does not fall from palm trees, even the ones swaying over Nobu in Cabo.

### A Parent's Quiet Investment

At the end of the day, money is just another part of the college learning curve. There are classes in calculus and creative writing, but the real test might be how they handle a budget, a credit card, or the urge to DoorDash a $6 Insomnia cookie at midnight because "I had a long day."

Letting them take more ownership with each semester was part of the plan. We didn't hand over the reins all at once, but we loosened our grip, little by little, until they had to steer.

Because somewhere between the quizzes, football games, roommate drama, and ramen nights, they're learning a skill that'll serve them long after the tassel turns: how to live within their means and still make it meaningful.

CHAPTER FOURTEEN

# Are They Thriving or Just Holding it Together?

At some point, usually after midterms, you start to wonder: are they okay? Not just "going to class" okay, but actually okay.

There's a strange space between over-parenting and staying too far removed. It's the gray zone where college parents quietly panic and wonder: "Are they doing okay?"

And the answer is… probably. But also? They won't always tell you.

Sometimes they don't want to worry you. Sometimes they don't know how to put it into words yet. And sometimes, they're just not in the mood for a deep dive over FaceTime.

**The Grade Check Dilemma**

You want to ask. You want to know. But asking "How are your grades?" every time you talk can make you sound like a guidance counselor with control issues.

We've all been tempted to ask, "You're going to class, right?" when the only thing they mention is intramurals, parties and a weird new energy drink.

If you have access to their student portal, use it sparingly. Most schools use two-factor authentication, which means your kid will know when you're logging in because the code goes to their phone. Trust goes both ways. And if you don't have access, that's okay too. Try asking something more open-ended like, "How are you feeling about your classes this semester?" or "What's been the toughest assignment so far?" Those kinds of questions create room for conversation, not shutdowns.

And let's be honest, sometimes the tone in their voice tells you more than the words ever could.

> **Mom's Take:** Moms tend to pick up on the vibe faster. We just do. Dads notice too, but sometimes it's one suspicious bank charge at a time. That subtle pause when they say "It's fine," or the lack of enthusiasm when they talk about class, it hits different. You start noticing patterns. The late responses, the vague updates, the calls that drop off mid-sentence. That's when the radar kicks in.

> **Mom's Pro Tip:** The first semester is a learning curve. Dual credit community college classes in high school helped ours prepare. Using tutoring or writing support services can make a big difference.

**Look for the Subtle Signs**

Not every struggle shows up with flashing lights. Sometimes it's a slow drip of changes:

Are they calling more… or not at all?

Are their texts upbeat, or a little off?

Are they suddenly unsure about their major or casually talking about transferring?

College is full of academic and emotional curveballs. One bad grade doesn't mean a spiral, but silence after midterms might be a flag worth checking in on. You don't need to interrogate. Just reach out with curiosity instead of judgment.

**Roommate + Social Red Flags**

Social dynamics can be as stressful as academics. Maybe more.

If they mention dorm tension, roommate drama, or feeling like they don't have a group, listen. Everyone feels lost at some point, especially during the first year. The key is whether they're figuring out how to move forward… or starting to disappear into isolation.

It's okay to ask, "That sounds rough. Want to talk through it?" You're not trying to solve it, just offer a sounding board.

And if the conversation starts edging into stress, sadness, or anxiety, don't brush it off with "You'll be fine." That might've worked in high school. Now, it can come across as dismissive.

Normalize help. Suggest the campus counseling center. If they're hesitant, remind them that going once doesn't mean committing to a year of therapy. It just means taking a step.

**Your Job Isn't to Solve, Just to See**

You don't have to fix it. You just have to notice.

Ask thoughtful questions. Let silence happen sometimes. Resist the urge to fill every pause with advice. The goal isn't to prevent every hard thing. It's to be someone they trust to call when it happens.

Because sometimes they won't say "I need help." They'll just say "I'm tired."

And if you've been paying attention, you'll know the difference.

> **Mom's Take:** I used to ask too many questions. I thought that's what a caring mom did. Check in, follow up, dig a little deeper. But eventually, I learned something that changed everything: if you just listen, they'll fill in the blanks. If you stay quiet long enough, they'll talk and keep talking until they're done.
>
> Those calls usually came around 11pm, just when I was ready to go to bed for work the next morning. But I took them anyway. Because once that window closes, it rarely reopens. They won't pick the conversation back up tomorrow. You have to be present when the door's open, even if you're tired. Especially then.

CHAPTER FIFTEEN

# Spring Break, Study Abroad and Other Budget Curveballs

Just when you think the spending has finally leveled out, here comes the next round: spring break, study abroad, and "a summer internship in another city." The curveballs don't stop, they just get more creative.

**Spring Break Shenanigans**

This one hits around February. Right when you're still recovering from holiday bills, they casually float the idea of Cabo, PCB, The Keys or Fort Lauderdale. Suddenly it's, "Everyone's going," and "We already found a cheap Airbnb!" which is college-student code for "We haven't booked anything and need money."

Do you fund it? That's up to you. Our rule was pretty simple:

If they planned for it and saved up, great.

If it was a last-minute ask with a big price tag? Hard pass.

You can support the fun without becoming the travel agent and financial backer. A little spending money? Sure. Covering flights, wristbands, hotel, and matching tanks for the whole group? Not happening.

> **Dad's Pro Tip:** If it starts with "Everyone's going," it usually ends with me checking flights, crunching numbers, and saying no. Fun is great, but your lack of planning is not a funding emergency. And honestly, part of growing up is realizing that not every trip or concert or last-minute plan is going to happen. They hate hearing that in the moment, but later they get it, and sometimes those no's are the lessons that stick.

> **Mom's Reminder:** It's easy to want to say yes when you're just happy they want to include you in the planning. But part of parenting through college is knowing when to smile and say, "Sounds amazing. Let me know how you're going to pay for it."

**Study Abroad = Study Budget**

The idea of studying abroad is dreamy. Italy. Spain. Australia. New experiences, cultural immersion, and the chance to Instagram from somewhere with better architecture. And we're all for it, if it makes sense.

What doesn't always show up in the brochure:

Flights, housing, food, weekend travel, international health insurance, visa fees, and the "I couldn't pass up this once-in-a-lifetime trip to Greece" side excursions. And don't forget, you will go to move them in as well. Or at least visit while they are there. You can't miss that.

If they're serious about going, treat it like a shared project:

- Break down the full cost together
- Look into program-specific scholarships or financial aid options
- Get clear on what you're willing to contribute, and what's on them

Even if they don't end up going, just walking through the numbers together is valuable. It teaches them how to weigh excitement against expense, how to want something and also understand what it takes to make it happen.

And if now's not the right time? That's okay. Study abroad isn't the only path. There are mini-semester programs, summer sessions, and post-grad travel opportunities that can still scratch that international itch without blowing up the college budget.

> **Mom's Take:** We were ready to support our daughter who wanted to study abroad. She'd narrowed the location, started making the plans, and we were behind her 100%. But then, she met someone. And little by little, the allure became less of a priority. She shifted her focus. I'm not sure she regrets it, but I know it changed her college experience. The relationship didn't last, but the decision did. And that's part of growing up too, learning what you really want, and what you're willing to let go of.

### Surprise Curveballs

Here's a quick list of things we didn't budget for, but definitely ended up paying for:

- A spring sublease and mid-year apartment move when our daughter backed out of a study abroad program
- Parking tickets (some earned, some... debatable)
- A lost dorm key that somehow required a full lock change
- One of their cars getting hit in the campus parking lot, no witnesses and no cameras to be found. The police checked, came up empty, and we had to run it through our insurance.

And if you've got a daughter like ours at Mizzou, who managed to live in at least seven different places during college, you learn pretty quickly: the surprises aren't if, but when.

These things pile up fast. Set up a system for how and when money gets transferred, and stay clear on what you'll cover versus what's on them. A recurring "Oops" fee isn't your responsibility forever.

### 21st Birthdays & Other "Adult" Moments That Still Matter

You think you are in the clear once they turn 18. But 21 is the real milestone. Especially for girls, whose 21st birthdays come with themes, bar crawls, photo shoots, and something called a "sign party," which you will pretend to understand.

Our twin daughters turned 21 in June, so school was out and both came home to celebrate. We spent the day in Chicago with rooftops, cocktails, and the whole deal, and it felt special to share it together. When the new semester rolled around, their friends made sure they didn't miss out on the tradition, throwing full-blown sign parties to make it official. Their birthdays may not have landed during the school year, but college kids never need an excuse to celebrate. They just found a reason to do it a few months late.

If your kid is in Greek life or a social group, expect to be asked to contribute to their "birthday book." You will get very specific instructions to create a full page with memories, photos, a cute note, and maybe a quote if you are lucky. It is like scrapbooking with a deadline and judgment. Just follow the template and remember, it is not about you. It is about being included.

Our son? Way easier. No theme. No sign. Just, "Want to come take me to dinner and grab a drink at midnight?"

We drove to Iowa City in the middle of the week, took him out, and grabbed a hotel for the night. It was not exactly cheap, but that first college birthday carried a little extra emotion, and we wanted to be there for it. After that, you do your best to keep showing up in ways that feel fair, even when every kid and every moment calls for something different.

There is no official rulebook for parental fairness. But you keep mental score. You check your gut. And you try to show up however you can.

### When a Weekend Visit Put Everything in Perspective

Not all surprises are good ones. On a long weekend visit to Tuscaloosa, my wife suddenly got very sick. The doctors first suspected a kidney stone, something she had never experienced before. They gave her morphine for the pain, sent us back to the hotel with more painkillers, and told me to watch for a fever. Hours later her fever spiked, and I found myself running red lights to get her back to the hospital. She was extremely sick. The doctors decided to put in a stent for the kidney stone, but when they did, it stirred up a nest of infection that had built in her kidney and pushed it into her bloodstream, sending her into septic shock. Only later did we learn she also had Influenza B and a UTI, the perfect storm that had escalated into full-blown sepsis.

What was supposed to be a quick three-day visit turned into a week in the hospital, including several days in the ICU.

Suddenly, I was navigating doctors, specialists, a hospital we didn't know, and medical decisions in a completely unfamiliar place. I had to extend our hotel stay, the car rental, and eventually got hit with the same strain of flu myself. Fever, chills, the works. Thankfully, some fellow parents-turned-friends let me stay in their nearby condo for a few nights. That bit of comfort meant more than they probably realized.

Our daughter stepped up in a huge way. She stayed calm, helped care for her mom, and later helped me get her home when we were finally cleared to travel. Her sister from Mizzou drove back home once we returned. One of my clearest memories is seeing the three of them sitting together on the bed, chatting quietly while my wife rested. That moment hit me. Life is fragile. Family matters more than anything. And sometimes your kids surprise you with just how strong they really are.

We were lucky. She fully recovered, though the pace of life stayed slow for a while. But that week shifted things. It reminded us of what is truly important and how quickly everything can change.

**A Quiet Sacrifice That Saved Us Thousands**

Our daughter at Mizzou stayed through the summer after freshman year and worked at a country club, just to make $2,000. Why? Because if she did and didn't leave the state for more than 14 days, she'd qualify for in-state residency. This decision and effort would cut her tuition in half from sophomore year through graduation. We're forever grateful she made that choice.

But the timing wasn't exactly ideal. A breakup made things uncomfortable in her friend group, and even though many of them were still in town, it didn't feel like she could be around them. She stuck it out, like she always does. This is our no-drama daughter. The one who never has a bad thing to say about anyone. Always sees the good. Hates confrontation. But we could tell she was hurting.

And the job? That wasn't easy either. Some guests at the country club were over the top demanding. Tips were inconsistent. She learned fast that working in service doesn't necessarily mean being treated with respect.

We did what we could from six hours away. Encouragement, check-ins, support. She didn't complain. She got through it. Quietly. That summer showed us what we already knew: she's tougher than she lets on and stronger than we ever gave her credit for.

And because she did that, because she made that choice and stuck with it, we didn't ask her to take out any loans the rest of the way through. We covered it. That felt fair. She earned that in-state status, and we were proud to back her the rest of the way.

These aren't just costs. They're choices. And each one is a chance to teach:

- How to plan ahead
- How to say no when the group says yes
- How to take responsibility without shame

Because one day, they'll have a job, a 401(k), and their own spring break regrets to fund.

And when that day comes, you'll be glad you helped set the tone early with love, limits, and maybe a little leftover Cabo envy.

And if they ever thank you for your financial restraint? Screenshot it. That's a unicorn moment.

## CHAPTER SIXTEEN

# When the Nest Is Half Empty (or Full of Laundry Again)

The day you officially become an empty nester feels both sudden and slow. One minute you're knee-deep in move-in bins and money transfers. The next, the house is quiet. The driveway is clear. And your fridge is finally under control. No mystery containers, no vanishing snacks, and everything right where you put it.

You don't quite know what to do with yourself.

For us, it happened gradually. When our son left, we still had the girls at home. The rhythm shifted, but we still had noise. When the twins left, within days of one another, that was the turning point.

No more Target runs for last-minute school projects. No more cheer competitions. No more coordinating five dinner schedules and trying to guess who was actually home that night.

Just… us.

> **Mom's Point of View:** I remember folding towels in silence one afternoon and realizing I didn't need to rush. The days of making lunches or checking on homework or reminding anyone about practice had long passed. I missed them, but I also felt something I hadn't in years: permission to rest. No one tells you this, but it's true, the quiet hurts, but it heals too. The house did feel empty, but eventually, it became something else. A place to breathe. A place to rediscover your partner. A place to miss your kids without drowning in it.

**The Laundry Mirage**

They come home. They visit. And when they do, it's like time reverses by five years in twenty minutes.

Shoes pile up by the back door. Water bottles, both empty and half full, multiply on the kitchen counter. The laundry they "promise they'll do tomorrow" lives in the mudroom for three days and then gets washed with your stuff anyway. You buy extra food and snacks. You lose your spot on the couch. You find one kid asleep in the basement with the TV still on and the mess they made somehow feels like a monument, as if it should be toured and photographed for years to come.

> **Dad's Pro Tip:** When they come home, expect the house to take a hit. The basement won't get cleaned up. The laundry room will look like a shoe explosion. Water bottles, half full and never capped, will multiply. The sink will be full, the dishwasher somehow empty, as if they never learned how it all works. Or worse, they'll load the dishwasher right

> on top of the clean dishes. Why check if they are clean? They'll sleep till noon, stay up all night, and leave behind just enough mess to remind you they were definitely here. You'll grumble. And then… you'll miss it.

It's annoying. It's beautiful. It's everything all at once.

And then… they leave again.

So you reset. Again.

There's a grief in that, one that hits softer each time but never fully disappears. And still, you find your way back to center. The space that felt so strange at first starts to feel like your own again.

This chapter is less about parenting them and more about tending to yourself, your marriage, your identity, your time.

Because as much as college is shaping them, this season is reshaping you too.

You start finding new rhythms. New hobbies. New goals. You start planning trips without working around three different class schedules. You get used to drinking your coffee while it is still hot.

At some point, the Life360 checks faded. What used to be a morning routine quietly disappeared, mostly for my wife, who had the app open more than her weather app. But over time, even she stopped refreshing it. For the first time in a long time, we did not need to know where everyone was. We just trusted they were okay. And we were okay too.

You finally have space. And in that space, you remember: they're okay. You're okay. And you're just getting started, too.

With a fridge and pantry that's a little less crowded, laundry that's manageable, and a spot on the couch that's all your own.

## CHAPTER SEVENTEEN

# Rediscovering Yourself (and Your Spouse)

After years of dance recitals, baseball and basketball tournaments, cheer competitions, coaching, and keeping a full fridge for a small army, you wake up one day and realize, it's just you again.

No more driving to practice. No more waiting up. No more dinners revolving around everyone else's schedule. Just two people in a quieter house, trying to remember what life felt like before you lived by a team calendar and a group chat.

> **Dad's Take:** I'll admit, the quiet caught me off guard. I didn't hate it, but it was strange. For so long, everything revolved around keeping up: who had what, where, and when. Most nights, we were prepping dinner for five without knowing if anyone was actually eating. Their plans were barely communicated or buried under so much noise we'd miss them

> anyway. Then suddenly, the house was still. The fridge stayed predictable. The nights opened up. So we leaned into it. We started dating again. Same kitchen, same couple, just fewer schedules and way more peace.

And for the first time in a long time, you get to ask: What do I want to do tonight?

For us, it started with food. Going out to dinner wasn't just a break from cooking, it was therapy. It was reconnection. It was a way to sit across from each other without laundry buzzing in the background or someone texting for ride. It reminded us of who we were before we were referees, chauffeurs, and 24/7 parents.

We didn't make some grand plan. We just started doing small things again.

Evening walks. Working out. Hitting the sauna. Picking up golf. Binge-watching shows during those winter months when the house felt especially still. Sharing a drink on the deck. Talking about where we'd want to travel next. Not for a tournament or a college visit, but just for us.

> **Mom's Point of View:** It wasn't instant. You think the quiet will feel like freedom, but at first it feels more like loss. I had to unlearn the urgency. No one was waiting on me to fix or manage or remind. The harder part was realizing I still mattered, even when I wasn't needed every minute of the day. That shift surprised me with how powerful it felt once I let it sink in.

### A Shift in Focus

Your life starts to open back up. Maybe it's:

- Finally finishing that house project
- Volunteering
- Learning something new
- Investing in your health
- Catching up with friends you've only texted the last four years

Whatever it is, it feels different now. A little bittersweet. A lot freeing.

You realize that the habits you built as a parent, being dependable, showing up, staying steady, still matter. You're just turning them inward now. Toward yourself. Toward your own growth. Toward the relationship that often got the leftovers.

And toward your spouse.

Because here's the honest truth: if you've spent years prioritizing everyone else, rediscovering each other isn't always automatic. There's no fanfare. It takes time. Intention. And a little space to remember how to enjoy each other's company without the parenting playbook running in the background.

But eventually, it clicks. The pressure lifts. You start laughing more. Talking more. Finding a rhythm again. Dreaming a little. Planning trips for fun, not for logistics. And somewhere in the middle of all that you find your way back to each other.

It doesn't mean you're done being parents. It just means you're allowed to be more than that now.

And you've earned it.

**Mom's Take:** The truth is, it isn't about filling the time, it's about reclaiming it. I started saying yes to small things for myself: longer walks, more time reading, reaching out to old friends I'd only texted in passing. I let go of that old version of "busy" and realized this season is mine too. It gave me peace, some joy, and even a little spark I didn't know I was missing.

CHAPTER EIGHTEEN

# A Note for Graduation (It Comes Sooner Than You Think)

You blink, and somehow, it's senior year.

You were just figuring out how to pack a dorm bin without forgetting the surge protector, and now you're trying to find a dinner reservation for twelve family members in a college town where supply and demand completely fall apart on graduation weekend.

Graduation hits differently.

It's pride and disbelief. Relief and nostalgia. A victory lap for them, and honestly, for you.

You'll go. You may cry. You will definitely celebrate. Tuition is over. You'll take 417 photos of them in their gown from every possible angle, then more with their friends. You'll buy the overpriced diploma frame from the bookstore, maybe an alumni license plate holder or sweatshirt, and pretend you're not doing the math in your head of what all this cost.

And then… they'll walk across the stage.

They'll wave. You'll look for them on the big screen. You'll cheer louder than you expected. And when you catch that glimpse of the cap, the grin, their final walk as a student that somehow grew up overnight, it'll hit you. They did it. You did it.

## What You're Really Celebrating

Then comes the dinner. The family. The toast. There's always a toast.

We gave one for all three of our kids. It didn't have to be perfect. It didn't have to be long. Just heartfelt. Just enough to mark the moment, say the thing, and let them know how proud we were. Not just of the degree, but of who they became on the way there.

> **Mom's Point of View:** For me, graduation was never just a ceremony. It was a collage of everything that came before it. I saw our son in his tiny football jersey at age ten. I saw our daughter packing for college, crying and pretending not to. I saw every Target run, every teary goodbye in a parking lot, every moment I had to let them figure it out without stepping in. And now, here they were, grown, grinning, and walking into their next chapter like they belonged there.

At some point, when the noise dies down and the group texts fade, you'll sit with that feeling. You'll think about all the firsts that led to this:

The first time they moved into a dorm

The first call home that made you worry

The first tailgate, the first test, the first heartbreak

The first time you realized they didn't need you, but still wanted to talk

You'll realize it was never about doing it perfectly. It was about showing up. Being there. Cheering, texting, moving, paying, trusting, listening, hoping, letting go, but never really leaving them.

> **Dad's Take:** It's not just the diploma that costs money. It's the final move, the dinners, the "they deserve it" splurges. We bought watches and earrings as keepsakes instead of handing out cash. Felt more personal. Also felt like a parting gift from us to them: "You did it. We saw it. We're proud." That's what it was always about, anyway.
>
> And remember those bag boards we purchased for their high school graduation parties? We saved them. After each college graduation, we gave them to the kids, school logos, team colors and all. A little piece of home. A lot of memories. And something they can take with them wherever they go next.

It hit me after the final graduation: "M-I-Z… Z-O-U," "Roll Tide," and "Go Hawks" weren't just cheers anymore. They were part of our family vocabulary, little echoes of the years spent in each place.

Graduation isn't the end of your role. It's just the start of a different one.

From here, the questions get bigger. The help gets subtler. The pride gets even deeper.

And your kid?

They'll always be yours. Just now with a tassel turned, a future ahead, and the confidence that comes from being loved all the way there.

Congrats, Parent. You graduated too.

You raised someone ready.

# EPILOGUE: HERE'S TO THE NEXT CHAPTER

Six years.

That's all it took to go from our first dorm drop-off to our last college graduation. In between, we packed more bins than we can count, signed leases we would never live in, hosted tailgates in three different towns, and spent enough at Target to deserve our own parking spot. We watched our kids go from high school seniors to young adults ready to build lives of their own. Somewhere in the middle, we figured out how to build ours, too.

We've been the bank, the moving crew, the pep-talk givers, and sometimes the comic relief. College parenting turned out to be equal parts pride, patience, and pretending you're fine when you're not.

There were moments that took our breath away. The first wave from the dorm steps. The first introductions to friends who became family. The first walk across the graduation stage. There were also moments that tested our patience, our budgets, and our ability to keep a straight face in a college bar. We loved them all, even the messy ones.

And now, the kids are off building their lives. And so are we. Maybe into an emptier nest. Maybe into new hobbies, travel, or rediscovering who we were before booster meetings and back-to-school nights. Whatever it is, it's the next chapter.

So here's to every mile, every memory, and every moment we got to be part of. Because college wasn't just their story.

It was ours, too.

# ACKNOWLEDGMENTS

This book wouldn't exist without the people who lived it with us.

To our three kids, Braeden, Brynn, and Braxtyn, thank you for giving us the stories, the material, and the memories that filled these pages. You taught us how to let go, how to stay connected, and how to survive a tailgate in all weather. Even when you didn't know it, you were shaping the lessons in this book.

To our family and friends who shared in the graduation parties, the moving days, the late-night calls, and the "just one more drink" game plans, thank you for the laughs, the extra muscle, and the reminders that this parenting chapter is better when it's shared.

To the fellow parents we met along the way in Iowa City, Tuscaloosa, and Columbia, thank you for welcoming us into your tailgates, splitting the setup and the costs more times than we can count, meeting us out for dinners and drinks after long game days, and sharing in traditions that made these weekends something to look forward to. Thank you for the times you opened your condo to us when life threw us a bigger curveball in Tuscaloosa than any tailgate or move-in, for lending us tools at a moment's notice, and for stepping in with the kind of help you can't order from Amazon. To the parents who coordinated splitting utilities or took them on for the semester and settled up at the end, you were the unsung heroes of off-campus living.

You reminded us that college parenting has its own tribe, and we're grateful we got to be part of it.

To the towns that welcomed us like locals: Go Hawks, Roll Tide, and M-I-Z... Z-O-U!

To the friends who encouraged us to write this, and to those who kept saying, "You should really put this in a book," thank you. You planted the seed that became these pages. Some of you even pulled up a chair, or a cooler, at our tailgates, kid in college or not, and made the stories better just by being part of them.

To the team who helped bring this to life, including our editor, designers, and early readers like Julie Kuss, thank you for your encouragement, your perspective, and for helping us shape these stories into something worth sharing.

And to the people who gently told us when a story was "funny for us, maybe less so for the reader," thank you for making this sharper, cleaner, and even more fun to read.

And finally, to every parent holding back tears in a dorm parking lot or cheering in a stadium miles from home, we see you, we're with you, and we hope these pages make the ride a little easier and a lot more memorable.

www.ingramcontent.com/pod-product-compliance
Ingram Content Group UK Ltd.
Pitfield, Milton Keynes, MK11 3LW, UK
UKHW042016190726
13854UKWH00005B/2314

9 798995 851509